CONTEMPORARY CHRISTIAN MORALITY

D1113228

RICHARD C. SPARKS, C.S.P.

CONTEMPORARY CHRISTIAN MORALITY

Real Questions,
Candid Responses

A Crossroad Herder Book
The Crossroad Publishing Company
New York

This printing: 2004

The Crossroad Publishing Company
16 Penn Plaza, 481 Eighth Avenue, New York, NY 10001

Copyright © 1996 by Richard C. Sparks, C.S.P.

All rights reserved. No part of this book may be reproduced, stored in a retrieval system, or transmitted, in any form or by any means, electronic, mechanical, photocopying, recording, or otherwise, without the written permission of The Crossroad Publishing Company.

All scriptural quotations are taken from the New Revised Standard Version Bible (1989).

Printed in the United States of America

Library of Congress Cataloging-in-Publication Data

Sparks, Richard C., 1950–
    Contemporary Christian morality : real questions, candid responses
/ Richard C. Sparks.
        p.   cm.
    ISBN 0-8245-1578-1 (pbk.)
    1. Christian ethics—Catholic authors—Miscellanea.   I. Title.
BJ1249.S634   1996
241'.042—dc20   95-51420
                                                                      CIP

Dedicated with love to my mother,

Margaret Mary (McFadden) Sparks,

on the occasion of her eightieth birthday.

Contents

Part Two
ISSUES IN HEALTHCARE ETHICS
(Questions 21–40)

Part Three
ISSUES IN SEXUAL MORALITY
(Questions 41–60)

Part Four
ISSUES IN POLITICAL AND ECONOMIC LIFE
(Questions 61–80)

Part Five
ISSUES IN PEACEMAKING, CAPITAL PUNISHMENT,
AND VIOLENCE
(Questions 81–95)

Preface

In the Hebrew Scriptures, we find God's fundamental challenge to the chosen people:

> I have set before you life and death, blessings and curses. Choose life that you and your descendants may live, loving the Lord your God, obeying him, and holding fast to him; for that means life to you and length of days. (Deut. 30:19–20)

Morality is about that fundamental choice, standing up for life rather than death, the path of blessing rather than curses, growth rather than stagnation. Morality is about the daily *how* of living life humanely and well. People all over the world make life choices, big and small decisions that impact their well-being and the good of the communities in which they live. One need not belong to any particular religion in order to make reasonable and humane choices about how to live a good life, a decent life, a moral life.

But the focus of this book in not morality in general, nor the often admirable moral codes of those who profess other creeds. *Christian* morality attests that for us who call ourselves "Christian," life lived abundantly well is life lived through, with, and in Christ Jesus. Jesus seemed to be responding to the ancient challenge quoted above when he proclaimed, "I came that you may have life, and have it abundantly" (John 10:10). Or in another place, he declared, "I am the way, and the truth, and the life" (John 14:6).

Christian morality is about a "we," not just a "me," facing life's fundamental choices. We are never alone in facing the choice to do

good or evil. We are never alone in our successes or our failures. It is
our Christian belief that Christ, in the Spirit, lives on in us as individuals and as the community called "the church." We are a community of fellow believers, a pilgrim people, called to journey
through life making a difference. How we live, how we love, and
how well we keep our commitments—these should be earmarks of
Christian individuals and our church communities. Jesus called this
hoped-for better world the "reign of God." It is the first stage of
God's eternal kingdom coming, as we pray in the Lord's Prayer.

This book is about Christian morality, about doing the right
thing, avoiding evil, and being rooted in the life, death, and resurrection of Jesus of Nazareth. I come to this venture as a Christian, a
member of the Catholic branch of the church, and an ordained
priest in that tradition. Thus, I will frequently present the teachings
of my denomination. There is much wisdom in our two-thousand-
year heritage. However, this is a book written not solely for
Catholics but for all Christians. Lutherans, Methodists, Presbyterians, Episcopalians, Baptists, as well as members of the United
Church of Christ, Orthodox churches, and other denominations all
share the power and grace of the Christian story. Much of the time
our collective Christian wisdom converges and we agree about what
moral course is right or wrong. Still, where there is disagreement or
shades of differences, I have tried to present this diversity and ongoing dialogue fairly.

I hope you will find the questions and my responses honest,
engaging, and true to your own experience. May you discover
insights here that are helpful for your own personal life. Often you
will find that I confirm your own deeply held beliefs and convictions. But there may be times when my reflections will challenge
you to reconsider a piece of your moral puzzle. In those instances I
hope you are willing to reexamine your own views on a given moral
topic. In the end, you may choose to revise or refine your moral
stance. Or you may decide that I am off base or incorrect on one
issue or another. You may be right. None of us is perfect. No one's
moral compass is infallible all the time. I invite you to dialogue
with me.

These one hundred questions are very special to me. They are
culled from two decades of ministry, preaching, teaching, counseling, and, most of all, *listening*. Most of the time I travel around

North America as an itinerant speaker and workshop presenter. My topics at workshops or areas of expertise encompass the various issues dealt with in this book—moral decision making, healthcare ethics, sexual morality, politics, economics, peacemaking, domestic violence, and the virtues—such as faith, fidelity, and forgiveness. These questions are your questions, or at least the questions I hear from people like you in workshop after workshop. They are the honest moral concerns of real people trying to live life well, as Christians, as good human beings, as solid citizens and family members.

While the responses to these questions, for good or ill, are my own, I have not written these pages in a vacuum or an ivory tower. They reflect my own personal and pastoral struggle to understand what it means to be moral and to put that into practice, in my life and in my teaching.

I'm grateful to my own Paulist community, whose support during my years of study and ministry has been unflagging. Likewise, I'm grateful to the people of St. Meinrad Archabbey and schools in southern Indiana. It was their hospitality that made possible the sabbatical time I needed to read, reflect, and write this volume. Finally, four of my colleagues and friends—Russ Connors, Ron Hamel, Mark O'Keefe, and Susan Secker—each took the time to read an earlier draft of this book, offering helpful suggestions for refinement and revision. I am grateful for their collective wisdom. The book is much improved because of their insights. And so I invite you to turn the page and join me in an ethical dialogue. May we strive always to "choose life," wisely, faithfully, and well.

CONTEMPORARY CHRISTIAN MORALITY

PART ONE

Definitions and Moral Decision Making

Q. 1. What is morality?

Basically, morality has something to do with living life well. No, not so much materially well (as in being wealthy), but "living life well" as in living a good life, being an upright person, a man or woman or child of good character. I suggest this as our starting definition: *Morality is one's values, choices, and actions.*

The "one" in our definition can refer to an *individual*. For example, *you* have your own set of values and beliefs. According to these values, you make choices and act on them. So do I. So does the president of the United States, a business executive in Europe, a homemaker in South America, a farmer on the plains of Africa, a sailor off the coast of Asia, and a shepherd on a hillside in the Middle East. Everyone has his or her own set of values or moral standards by which to live.

The "one" in our definition can also refer to a *community*. We each belong to a variety of groups or communities, each with its own set of values, its own code of proper behavior. At one and the same time I am an American, a child of the sixties, Caucasian, middle-aged, male, a midwesterner, mostly Irish by descent, a member of the Sparks clan, a Christian, of the (Roman) Catholic tradition, single, and a priest. Just think about your own life. To how many different communities do you belong? Each of those groups has its own moral code, its own spoken or unspoken, written or merely intuited sense of what is right and what is wrong for people who belong to that community.

So, as we begin this one-hundred-question conversation, it's

1

important to realize that one's *morality* is a complex thing. Influenced by the variety of overlapping communities in which we live, ultimately each of us adopts our own hybrid morality. We each weave together, in an ongoing way, our own set of personal values and, hopefully, we try to be faithful to these core convictions as we make life choices and live them out.

Q. 2. Are "ethics" and "morality" the same thing?

Some moral theologians and professional ethicists make a big distinction between *ethics* and *morality*. They define ethics as the "theory" and morality as the "practice" of living morally good lives. Others would propose that morality and ethics are related to each other in the same way that plant life and botany are related, or numbers and mathematics. The first—morality, plant life, numbers—is the topic or content studied, while the second—ethics, botany, mathematics—is the thematic, systematic, reflective study of the first. Thus, *morality* is the human values, choices, and actions that are studied in a formal way in an *ethics* class or by someone trained as an *ethicist*.

However, a person may live a very good moral life and in that sense know "morality" very well but not be able to talk about it in any formal or sophisticated "ethical" way. One thinks of some senior citizens who have had little formal schooling and who never darkened the door of an ethics classroom. Yet they help their neighbors in need, face life's difficulties with a hopeful attitude, pray or go to church frequently, and live exemplary lives. They are truly good, morally upright people. At the same time, here and there one finds a professor of ethics who can name all the theories, put all the values and virtues in neat categories, but whose personal life is anything but exemplary. Ideally, one's study of ethics ought to impact one's moral behavior. But *knowing about* something and *actually doing* it are not always synonymous. While there is some merit to this *ethics* versus *morality* distinction, in everyday speech the two terms are often used interchangeably. One's values, choices, and actions are called by some one's "morality" and by others, one's "ethics."

Q. 3. **If every person and every group has his, her, or its own "morality," then is everything relative? Mine is right for me, yours for you, and never the twain shall meet.**

At first glance it might seem so. Certainly one gets the impression that our pluralistic society, with its "do your own thing" mind-set of recent decades, has adopted *relativism* as its moral standard. But the Christian tradition tells us that just because one has a morality, a set of values according to which one makes choices and acts, he or she may not be choosing wisely or well. In other words, we believe that there is such a thing as *objective morality*. By "objective" I mean that there is a way life ought to be lived and a way it shouldn't. The fact that most of us think, all things being equal, that we ought to be honest, fair, kind, forgiving, and merciful is not merely a coincidence. Whether one speaks of it as God's will or as the way Nature or the Fates meant it to be or as what is reasonable to thoughtful human beings, people in various times and places adopt many of the same values as central and choose to live and act accordingly.

Many of these underlying values are taken for granted. When you ask someone for directions, you generally expect that he or she will give you a straight answer, the truth as best they know it. When you pay someone a decent wage or a fair price for a product, you expect that she or he will do a reasonable day's work or give you a decent product in exchange. Living with others would be extremely difficult if, as in some *Star Trek* episodes, the world were turned upside down morally speaking. If everyone lied, cheated, stole, murdered, and plundered their neighbor, then we would live in a constant state of suspicion, guardedness, and probably warlike hostility. As it is, we believe there is some objective standard of right and wrong, the way things are meant to be—by God, by nature, by human reason.

Moreover, in some moral situations there may be several objectively right choices, any of which one may freely choose. Our moral choice may be the lesser of two evils or the greater good among a variety of viable alternatives. Our belief in objective morality does not necessarily guarantee that the choice will be black and white, or squarely between two options, one clearly moral and the other patently immoral.

Q.   **4. How do we figure out whose values, choices, and actions ought to be the standard for all, the measure of this "objective morality" that you propose?**

That is a good question and not an easy one to answer in a sentence or two. Some suggest that we find a Bible text that speaks about a given moral issue, lift it out of its context of twenty to thirty centuries ago, and drop it on a twentieth-century problem as a ready-made, timeless answer. For example, the fifth commandment says, "Thou shalt not kill." So one might simply conclude that all taking of life, whether in war or peace, of criminals or of the innocent, in self-defense or not, is absolutely immoral—end of discussion. While a world free of all violence and killing would be a wonderful thing, most of us see the flaw in such a literal use of scripture. The commandment against killing was never seen, even by the Israelites, as a prohibition of all killing. Certain boundaries were established to distinguish between immoral, wrongful killing and other taking of life that might be tragic and regrettable but in some limited instances morally defensible. So the Bible is one viable source for morality, but it is not always applicable in a literal or fundamentalistic way. We'll come back to the role of the Bible for moral decision making in a later question.

Others suggest that human reason can figure out moral truth. Whether one calls it natural law, or folk wisdom, or prudence, or maybe even common sense, there is something in the mind and heart of all people that can intuit and reason *what ought to be*, based on an honest look at the *way things are*. Then can everyone decide moral right and wrong perfectly? Is our human logic flawless and infallible? Obviously not. Even with the best of intentions we all make mistakes. But there does seem to be a wisdom or a potential for wisdom at the core of the human spirit that can discover what it means to be a good person and what a flourishing human community might look like. We've glimpsed it and tasted it in our own lives in moments of love and community service. We can envision it as the way things *ought to be*, not only for me or you but for all people who seek a good life, a better world.

Q. **5. If the Bible doesn't have all the answers, at least not black and white, and if people can discover right from wrong just by thinking about it, then what is "Christian" about the morality Christians profess?**

There's been a debate going on among prominent Christian theologians about this very question. One group suggests that when it comes to specific actions and the kinds of values that move us to do or not to do those actions Christians have no corner on the market of moral knowledge. While the New Testament speaks about love of neighbor and forgiving someone many times over, one can also find similar wisdom in the Hebrew Scriptures (Old Testament), which Jews follow; in the Qur'an, which Muslims follow; in the scriptures of other world religions; and in the practical wisdom of many who have no particular religious faith. When it comes to *promoting* love, justice, forgiveness, mercy, and honesty or to *prohibiting* hatred, injustice, vengeance, holding a grudge, and lying, Christians have no special knowledge, nor do we practice these values with greater regularity than do many of our sisters and brothers of other faiths and philosophies of life.

Other theologians counter by stating that there seem to be some special duties or moral obligations connected with being a Christian that do not oblige non-Christians. For example, Christians ought to participate in the Lord's Supper, while those of other faiths are exempt. The gospel calls all followers of Jesus to be baptized in water and the Holy Spirit. These and other similar religious practices impose duties on Christians that seemingly do not oblige the wider human family.

Both schools of thought, however, acknowledge that the primary uniqueness of Christianity—or of any other faith tradition or life philosophy—is in the realm of story and worldview. That is where we must look to find what is distinctively "Christian" about Christian morality.

Q. **6. What do you mean by "story" or "worldview"?**

In our first question we noted that each person fashions his or her own moral values, choices, and actions from life experiences and from the various communities that are a part of that person's life. Parents, sisters and brothers, grandparents, other relatives and friends offer us our first glimpse into the meaning of life, shaping our underlying view of the world around us—whether life is basically good or bad, whether people are generally trustworthy or to be held at bay, and so on. How do they do this? By their actions, by their words, by the stories they tell and by whether they "practice what they preach." So too, our extended family and friends, our neighborhood, school, civic community, ethnic group, nation, *and our church* all play a part in helping to shape us, to make us who we are at any given point in our life's journey.

In the end, each of us must cull from all our life experiences and from the various communities in which we live the beliefs we will hold. Often this process of sifting, choosing, and committing oneself takes place during the teenage years or after one leaves home for the first time. So too, some people discover who they really are and what they truly believe while dating and coming to know their future spouse. This is the time when many people decide to join a church community, to rejoin the church of their youth, or to forgo specific religious or church commitments altogether. Each of us views life from the perspective of our own worldview—our values, our biases, our loves, our prejudices, our commitments, our fears— all culled from our own life experiences in the communities to which we belong. Usually one's core beliefs or those of a given community can be told in narrative or story fashion, highlighting what one believes about God, life, human nature, good and evil, and the meaning of it all. Across the centuries, we Christians have preserved and passed from one generation to the next our own treasured faith story.

Q. 7. What, then, is the Christian story?

The Christian story is about a relationship, a love relationship, an unconditional love affair between God and humanity. It culminates in the story of Jesus Christ—who he was, what he did, what he went through, and *who he still is,* for you and me, for all humanity. At the very dawn of creation God breathed on the waters and created life.

On the sixth day of the poetic story of creation God created humankind in God's own image, male and female, making us responsible for the whole world in all its wonder. Later God made a special pact of love, a *covenant* commitment, with the Jewish people, who came to be known as God's "chosen people." Over the centuries God has remained bonded with them in a special way, sending prophets and guiding them by revelation and commandments. Their checkered history of fidelity and mistakes is there for all to read in the Hebrew Scriptures (what Christians call the "Old Testament").

In miniature theirs is the story of God's abiding love for and fidelity with all people. We human beings straddle the seesaw of life, balancing between being basically good, lovable, made in the image and likeness of God and being sinners, self-centered, immature, not living up to the best that is within us. In a mysterious, almost unbelievable way, God so loves us for our goodness and is so willing to forgive our sinfulness, that God sent his only Son to become one of us.

This Jesus of Nazareth spent his life as an itinerant preacher, proclaiming God's healing love to all those in need. In the end, for a variety of self-serving reasons, the people arrested and crucified him. Even then, hanging nailed to a wooden cross, tempted to despair and to give up, Jesus asked God to forgive those who had crucified him and, by extension, to forgive all people. He yielded up his spirit and died, still pledging his fidelity to God and to those who believe in him. On the third day after this redemptive act of faithful love, Jesus Christ rose from the dead, demonstrating that even death cannot hold back God's power and mercy.

Within a short time God's Holy Spirit came upon the remnant of Jesus' followers, to inspire and encourage them, fulfilling Christ's pledge not to abandon them. In cooperation with this Spirit, in communion with Jesus the risen Christ, and under the protective care of God as "Father," the followers of Jesus gathered in faith (i.e., the church) live on across time and space, passing on Christ's message of love, trying to make real the reign of God, which Jesus inaugurated.

That, in rather sketchy fashion, is our Christian *story*. And it is out of this story, this faith experience of God's unconditional and abiding love for us, that we craft our view of life, our distinctively Christian *worldview*. Each denomination or Christian church refines the message a bit differently. Each of us imbues it with our own personal life experiences, but the basic story of God's abiding love and fidelity, of human sinfulness, and of Jesus' life-giving death and resurrection lives on. It colors how we who call ourselves Christians view ourselves, others, the world around us, and the meaning of it all.

Q. **8. You have summarized the Gospels and Christian creed clearly. But what does that have to do with our morality?**

Already built into the story of God's dealings with humanity, particularly the story of Jesus, we find some of the core values that Christians hold dear—love and fidelity, mercy and forgiveness, courage and fortitude. If we are made in the image and likeness of God, as the book of Genesis declares, and if we are called to be followers of Jesus, making his way of life our model for good living, then we ought also to be faithful in our commitments, loving and merciful to *all* people, not just to our friends or to those we think "deserve" it.

God cares about every person, about every living thing, not because we earn that love or *do* enough to please God, but just because we *are*. The starting point for Christian morality is our experience of and belief in God's gracious love before all else. God so loves us and is so anxious to help us and so willing to forgive us, that we ought to mirror that love and to pass that kind of unconditional care on to others.

So the Bible, especially the New Testament, is our Christian journal or family album. It contains the basic story of God's abiding love across the centuries, made even more tangible in the life, death, and resurrection of Jesus. From this story and from the other books and letters in the Bible, we discover the values that our ancestors in faith held dear. This "tradition" summons us, as their heirs in faith, to try to make real those same convictions in our choices and daily actions. So too the scriptures are full of very human stories of faith, of people such as Peter, Mary Magdalene, John the Baptist, Matthew the tax collector, Martha, Mary, and their brother Lazarus. Jesus himself was a storyteller. In his many parables and in the real-life encounters he had with various people—centurions, Pharisees, Samaritans, lepers—we discover the values he believed and taught.

The Bible is a rich source of stories, values, and illustrations of good living. It can serve as a primer for us in learning how to be people of faith and virtue—men, women, and children of good character.

So, to bring together questions 5–8, what makes Christian morality distinctive is the story of God's abiding love, made real and incarnate in Jesus Christ. His life, death, and resurrection are the pattern or pathway we all must follow. In good times and in bad, the values and virtues of the scriptures, especially the New Testament, chart a way for us. We are called to make real in our lives the same virtues and good character that are so evident in the life of the carpenter of Galilee.

Q. 9. What do you mean by "virtue" or "character"?

There was a time not too long ago, when Christian ethics, particularly in the Roman Catholic church, focused almost exclusively on the morality of specific actions, with a special emphasis on the negative. Is this or that action a sin? If so, is it a mortal or a venial sin? How many times did you do it? Did you repent of it? Did you confess it? The name of the game was actions. The emphasis was on sinful acts, and morality seemed to consist almost exclusively in *doing* or *not doing* certain deeds.

Beginning in the years after World War II and coming to fuller expression in Christian theology of the 1960s and 1970s, there has been increasing concern about what lies beneath or behind our choices to act in this or that way. Morality seems to be as much about *who we are* as about *what we do*. Another way of saying this is that who we are spills over into what we do (or don't do); and what we do, whether good or bad, tends to make us into the kind of persons we are. *Virtue* (or *character*) is the traditional name for the habit or practiced pattern of doing good and living life well. Its opposite, *vice*, is the term for a bad habit or the practice of doing evil, living a vicious (i.e., "viceful") or immoral way of life.

For example, if I say I believe in the value of honesty and if I practice telling the truth whenever I'm asked a question, then, as the old saying goes, "Practice makes perfect." Continued truth telling helps me to build within myself a pattern, a way of life, in which being honest is almost second nature. It comes naturally. Thus, *honesty* becomes one of my virtues. The next time someone asks me for a truthful answer, I don't have to think twice about it. Honesty is a value I esteem, a virtue or practiced pattern in my life, and I am naturally honest and forthright in my daily dealings with others.

Virtues—the individual elements of being a person of virtue or good character—can be packaged in a variety of ways or lists. Traditionally *faith, hope,* and *love* have been called the theological or infused virtues (see 1 Corinthians 13). *Prudence, justice, temperance,* and *fortitude* are known as the cardinal or moral virtues. University of Notre Dame professor Richard McBrien, in the recently revised edition of his book *Catholicism,* offers an interesting and helpful division. In terms of our relationship with God he suggests that *humility* and *gratitude* are virtues to be practiced. In dealing with our neighbors, we ought to cultivate *mercy* and *concern for the poor, forgiveness, justice,* and *truthfulness.* The world and environment in which we live benefit from our practice of good *stewardship.* And in terms of treating ourselves well, the virtues of *temperance* (i.e., moderation) and *fortitude* (i.e., commitment or courage over the long haul) are key. If each of us could develop and put these virtues into practice, we would truly be virtuous, people of good character.

Q. **10. When I was growing up, most sermons and religion classes on morality focused on sin, not on character or virtues. What is "sin"?**

In the scriptures the Greek word most frequently used for sin, *hamartia,* is an action term that refers to "missing the mark." If our lives are headed in a good and godly direction and by some conscious thought, word, or deed we get off target, move off the so-called straight and narrow, that willful mistake or "missing the mark" can be called sin. Many of us were raised with the model or metaphor of sin as disobedience, usually related to God's law or commandments. "Thou shalt not _____" was the usual form of the lists of sins we learned, whether the Ten Commandments or some longer list of dos and don'ts. Many contemporary theologians and preachers suggest another image, that of a love relationship. In this model, sin refers to those times when we fall short or "miss the mark" in being the kind of family member, spouse, friend, co-worker, citizen, or child of God that we ought to be.

We are each called to be responsible (i.e., to respond well) in the various relationships in our lives. When we do well, when we rise to the occasion, we can breathe easy and rejoice. Whether by virtue already present or by the struggle to become virtuous, we, with God's help, have triumphed. But when we act either irresponsibly or just fail to respond, we must admit that we have fallen short, missed the mark; we have sinned.

Part of the difficulty with "sin" language is that it has been used for a variety of related but distinct realities across the Christian tradition. Most of us have heard of the term *original sin*. It refers to the pride or selfishness of our first human parents in the mythical story of Adam and Eve. But their flaw—a deep-rooted tendency to miss the mark, to be self-centered, to see all of life focused on "me, myself, and I"—is not unique to them or to the Garden of Eden. There seems to be a streak of self-centeredness in each of us.

Another dimension of original sin is what some people call *social sin*. If an evil tendency is built into the social fabric of an entire community, as racism was built into South Africa during the decades of legalized apartheid, that systemic or community-wide evil is often called "sin" or "social sin" (see Q. 75). In one sense, no single person is responsible or to blame for it. But in a larger sense, each member of the community is more or less responsible for not seeing the evil and trying to root it out. Those who hold more power in the community are more accountable if social sin is tolerated and perpetuated.

Sin is also the term that scripture sometimes applies to all that is bad or unpleasant in life. The book of Genesis implies that illness, the pain of childbirth, having to earn our daily bread by the sweat of our brow, natural disasters, and even death are somehow related to "sin." Surely this does not mean that we are to blame for every negative event that befalls us. The story of Job, the innocent person who, through no fault of his own, suffered a series of tragic misfortunes, stands as a testimony to the fact that some kinds of evil, even if labeled "sin," have nothing to do with personal responsibility or blame.

Finally, and most correctly, *sin* refers to our personal human choices to do wrong, to choose the way of vice rather than the way

of virtue, to "miss the mark" when it comes to living out our commitments and responsibilities. Sin is this free-willed choice to do
moral evil. In the new *Catechism of the Catholic Church,* sin is defined
as an offense against reason, truth, and right conscience. Our failure to love God, neighbor, and ourselves as we should wounds us
and our social solidarity (#1849).

Q. 11. **Catholics make a big distinction between "mortal"
and "venial" sin, whereas most Protestants don't spend
much time putting sins into categories. Could you explain
this for me?**

One might say that the Roman Catholic tradition places greater
emphasis on *our role,* our human cooperation with God's grace in
bringing about God's reign here on earth, whereas the various
Protestant churches highlight *God's unmerited action* in redeeming
sinful humanity. Another way of saying this is that the Protestant
tradition emphasizes God's actions, primarily God's forgiving
actions (i.e., redemption or salvation), while Roman Catholicism
has tended to stress human actions, our graced capacity to respond
to God's gifts (i.e., empowerment or sanctification). It follows, then,
that Catholics would have a greater interest in analyzing human
actions, both the good and the bad, while most Protestants speak
more about God's graciousness and mercy.

Because of this, across the centuries Catholics have distinguished
between categories or kinds of sin and the seriousness or gravity of
various sinful actions. For example, murder seems to be a more serious sin than slapping someone in the face. Embezzling millions of
dollars seems to be a greater wrong than stealing a candy bar from
the corner store. Having sex with another person's spouse (i.e.,
adultery) seems to be more serious than winking at or flirting with
her or him. In common parlance people speak of the difference
between slander or a bald-faced lie and what some people call a fib
or a "white lie." In each instance the former action is more serious,
more deadly, more destructive of human relationships and of our
oneness with God than is the latter.

The term *mortal sin* has become the commonly accepted name
for grave sin, the kind of sin that destroys human bonds and,

according to the Catholic tradition, interrupts or even short-circuits our relationship with God. This in no way is intended to diminish God's abiding love for us, nor our belief that God's mercy exceeds strict justice. The concept of mortal sin is grounded in the fact that we do have free will, the ability to say yes or no in some definitive way to God's call to live good lives. In addition to the gravity of the action itself, one must fully understand the serious-ness of one's choice and freely choose it in order for such sin to be "mortal." *Venial sin* is the name given to less serious offenses against God, neighbor, or self. All of us are prone to commit these lesser or venial sins. They are the stuff of human frailty, foibles, and daily frustrations. They destroy neither our human bonds nor our rela-tionship with God.

Many suggest that dividing all sin into only two levels of gravity—mortal and venial—is an insufficient distinction that is too cut-and-dried. Some have suggested expanding the levels to include a middle category of *serious sin*, between the extremes of venial and mortal. The point of such discussions is not to create a tidy mathe-matical formula but to indicate the commonsense truth that some sins are more serious, more harmful to all concerned than others. So-called venial sins are more easily overlooked, corrected, and for-given, whereas so-called mortal sins cause more deadly harm and thus demand greater repentance, amendment, and satisfaction. Still, the *Catechism of the Catholic Church* cautions that even venial sin, if deliberate and unrepented, can dispose us little by little toward committing mortal sin (#1863). And with that we're back to the idea of virtue and vice, good and bad habits or life patterns, and the need to develop a healthy sense of conscience in all matters, whether slight, serious, or extremely grave.

Q. **12. You mentioned "conscience." Isn't "following your conscience" the real measure of morality?**

The most honest response is yes and no. Yes, we are obliged to fol-low our conscience, to do what we, at the very depth of our souls, believe is right. But no, that does not mean that we always discern accurately what is right versus what is wrong. In the end we are obliged to "follow our consciences," but with the caveat that we may or may not have discerned wisely and well. We have now returned to the issue of objective morality, which we first touched on in question 3.

A number of Christians mistakenly think of conscience as some magic voice inside our heads that automatically knows right from wrong, or perhaps a little devil on one shoulder and an angel on the other who temptingly whisper into our ears "Do it" or "Don't do it." Others believe that conscience is synonymous with guilt feelings. Not so. While a person with a well-formed sense of right and wrong may feel "guilty" when tempted to act sinfully, there is no guarantee that a person's guilt feelings are accurate. If one had been raised in South Africa prior to the last decade or so, a person might feel little guilt about apartheid. Indeed one might feel quite comfortable believing that white people are inherently better than people of color. In the reverse direction a person might have a neurotic or scrupulous sense of guilt, feeling inordinately responsible for things that are either not wrong or are beyond one's control.

Conscience is more of a verb than a noun. Conscience refers more to the process we go through in discerning right from wrong than to any particular organ or place or faculty within us. In the Old Testament we find the story of young King Solomon about to ascend the throne of his father David. God appears to Solomon in a dream and says, "Ask what I should give you." And in response, rather than seeking a long life for himself or riches or power over his enemies, young Solomon requests, "Give your servant therefore an understanding mind [some translations say 'an understanding heart'] to govern your people, able to discern between good and evil" (1 Kings 3:1–9). Yes, Solomon asked for wisdom, an understanding mind or heart, the ability to do "conscience" or moral discernment well. Another name for this might be the virtue called *prudence* or practical wisdom.

So conscience is not synonymous with intelligence in an academic sense, with book knowledge, or with ivory-tower wisdom. Rather, *conscience* is the ability to reason or discern well the moral decisions we face in our daily lives. Conscience is the innate yet practiced ability to determine what is morally good and right versus what is morally evil and wrong. St. Paul weaves together the notion of an understanding heart with the formal Greek word for conscience early in his letter to the Romans: "[Gentiles] show that what the law requires is written on their hearts, to which their own conscience also bears witness" (Rom. 2:15).

Across the Christian centuries the term *conscience* has been used for at least three different dimensions or levels of the moral decision-making process. First, one must have an understanding heart or mind, the basic ability to be able to discern good from evil. Most human beings have this capacity. Only those who have suffered massive brain damage or emotional trauma, or those who are severely retarded and thus unable to comprehend right and wrong can be said to lack a conscience or the ability to do the work of conscience. In the same way, people who are psychiatrically diagnosed to be sociopaths or psychopaths seem to lack the ability to differentiate right from wrong. Exempting these few people, the rest of us have the capacity to do conscience. In that sense we each "have" a conscience, the inner capacity to learn from our stories and life experiences, to reasonably discover right from wrong.

Second, throughout our lives we spend much time "informing our consciences," sensitizing and sharpening the values, practicing the virtues, and generally learning what it means to be persons of faith, commitment, integrity, maturity, and good will. Reading this book, for instance, is an exercise of this second dimension of conscience. As you read, you are not making any specific or major moral decisions. Rather, you are gathering information and insights about specific moral questions, which you might use later, either in your own moral decision making or in assisting others to decide wisely and well.

Third, the actual work of conscience, properly speaking, comes to the fore when we ourselves are faced with a moral dilemma. It may be a moral issue that is new to us, about which we have little prior knowledge or wisdom. Or it may be a moral question that we thought was clear in our minds but now becomes more cloudy when we face it personally. One thinks of complex biomedical issues like artificial insemination or *in vitro* fertilization as moral dilemmas that may confront childless married couples. This final conscience process takes place in the most secret and deepest sanctuary of a person—one's heart, mind, or soul. Like Mount Sinai, where Moses met God face to face, we ultimately make our conscience decisions in the silence of our own hearts, where God's voice echoes within.

When dealing with our own conscience process or that of another, it is wise to tread gently for we are standing on "holy ground."

Q. **13. But if we are obliged to follow our conscience, what happens if we make a mistake? Will we go to hell for it?**

That is a wonderful question and it brings us to a core distinction in the Christian tradition that is often overlooked in contemporary discussions of morality—the *objective* versus *subjective* distinction. In the end, after we have tried our best to discern wisely and well, we are obliged to do what our conscience decision tells us to do. Martin Luther is remembered well for his famous statement, "Here I stand, I can do no other." He was a person of integrity. While the leaders of the Roman Catholic church of his day were convinced that he was objectively wrong in a number of his theological opinions, he had tried, through prayer and serious study, to discern what he truly believed to be right. Once convinced, he felt he had to be true to his conscience. There he *must* stand, and "in good conscience" he could do nothing else.

A century earlier, in the 1400s, young Joan of Arc paid the ultimate price for her fidelity to conscience. Burned at the stake as a witch, she steadfastly refused to deny her faith in God, in her French homeland, and in her own inner convictions. This peasant teenager, the armored maid of Orleans, has inspired such agnostic curmudgeons as Mark Twain and George Bernard Shaw. She is a perennial favorite saint in popular piety as well as in literature, film, and the theater.

In the same way, in the sixteenth century, British nobleman Sir Thomas More was beheaded for defying Henry VIII, refusing to violate his conscience judgment about the morality of the king's multiple marriages. Having no "window to look into another man's conscience," he condemned no one. But he steadfastly refused to take an oath swearing agreement to something that he firmly held to be wrong. Playwright Robert Bolt calls him *A Man for All Seasons*, a symbol of that challenge in every age to be a woman, man, or child of integrity, true to one's conscience and conviction, whatever the consequences. In the play and film by the same name, Thomas More defines an oath as holding oneself in one's own hands, like a cupful of water. If we deny our own heartfelt convictions, then it is as if we open our fingers, allowing our very integrity to slip through and drain away.

Being a person of good conscience means being true to our own inner convictions and to our own internal decision-making process. Once we have decided that it is morally right or wrong to do something, then we are obliged to adhere to that conscience decision. We are *subjectively* sincere, even if we have inadvertently misread the *objective* rightness or wrongness of the situation. It is a core belief of the Christian tradition that God will judge us mercifully in such situations, not because our action was necessarily objectively correct but because in the sincerity of our hearts we strove to choose the good. To the extent that we didn't know any better, God accepts our *subjective* sincerity and we will not be held accountable for such mistakes. If, however, our failure to discern wisely and well is due to our own negligence or slipshod conscience process, then we are guilty to some degree, at least for our negligence, even if not for the full weight of our objectively immoral choice. Here too we must rely more on God's merciful understanding and forgiveness than on our assumed moral wisdom. Our task, in the meantime, is to try to discern as well as we can in our own lives, to be true to our conscience decisions, and to give others the same latitude and forgiveness that we hope and trust God will grant to us.

Q. **14. How does this *objective* versus *subjective* distinction work in our everyday moral discussions? It sounds as if it might be a way to rationalize "doing your own thing" and not being held accountable.**

On the contrary, I find that being aware of this distinction allows us to make more headway in moral discussions. If someone thinks that I am going to judge their sincerity, their interior state of soul, they will be much more likely to be defensive about their moral opinion on a given issue. However, if we all agree that we will not tread on a person's *subjective* sincerity, we will not violate anyone's conscientious good intention, then often we are freer to discuss moral questions in the *objective* arena. It is much easier to discuss why drug addiction is self-destructive and in that sense wrong, if I acknowledge up front that many or most substance-addicted people need our understanding and help, not our moral finger pointing. The old adage "Hate the sin but love the sinner" comes to mind here, though it might better be phrased "Hate the *objectively* immoral action, but love the person who may not be *subjectively* fully culpable for it."

Don't get me wrong. This is not intended to excuse everyone from responsibility for their own moral choices. We continually seek to bring together both objective moral rightness and our subjective discernment about that moral issue. Just as we strive to bring who we are into line with what we do, so also we strive to choose subjectively the objectively best course of action when facing moral dilemmas. The slang term "getting our act together" is apropos for doing well this conscience formation or moral discernment process.

Q. 15. How do we make a moral decision when facing a new or confusing moral dilemma?

In the middle of the thirteenth century, Thomas Aquinas, a Dominican scholar and saint, proposed a method for moral decision making that has been echoed, paralleled, and adopted in the succeeding centuries (*Summa Theologica* I,II, Q. 18). It is known as the *triple-font theory* because one must focus on three distinct components when discerning a moral question: (1) the act itself, (2) all the pertinent circumstances, and (3) the intention or mixed intentions of the person contemplating the act. In an insightful article entitled "Ethics: How to Do It," Marquette University professor Daniel Maguire further developed these three dimensions of moral decision making by asking eight key questions: What? Who/m? When? Where? How? Foreseeable Consequences? Viable Alternatives? Why(s)?

When facing a new or confusing moral question, it helps to look first at the action itself. *What* are we thinking of doing? Even before we add the circumstantial factors, a general judgment can be made that the act is initially good, bad, or neutral. For example, giving someone a pleasant object, all things being equal, would be good. Punching someone in the face, all things being equal, would be bad.

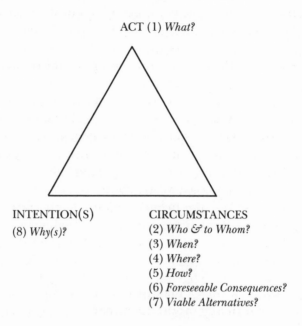

ACT (1) *What?*

INTENTION(S)
(8) *Why(s)?*

CIRCUMSTANCES
(2) *Who & to Whom?*
(3) *When?*
(4) *Where?*
(5) *How?*
(6) *Foreseeable Consequences?*
(7) *Viable Alternatives?*

And shouting "Hip, Hip, Hooray," all things being equal, would be neither good nor bad, but neutral. But one's moral discernment doesn't stop there.

Who is doing the act and *to whom?* In other words, who is the actor and who is the recipient (or the victim)? Whether the two are friends or foes and whether one has some justification for doing the deed to the other does make a difference. The act of sex, which we would judge to be "good" at the act level, remains positive if done by a loving married couple. It takes on quite a different value if it is sex violently forced upon another. We call such an act "rape," and it is never morally justified.

When and *where* is the action being done? For example, loading a gun at rush hour on a crowded city bus is quite a different matter from loading a rifle on the opening day of hunting season out in the woods. *How* one does a deed bespeaks the doer's attitude (e.g., conceited or humble) and is in some sense related to one's under-lying intention or motives.

The term *foreseeable consequences* raises the issue of responsibil-ity for the outcome, the various effects that my choice will have on others, not only those results that I desire but all anticipated side effects as well. Are there *viable alternatives?* If so, and if one or another of those is more fruitful or less harmful, then surely I would be obliged to take that course of action.

And finally, if this is a reasonably free choice on my part, then *why* am I choosing to do it? Our initial good action—giving someone a pleasant object—might be done as an expression of love or friendship. Giving a gift is a morally commendable thing to do. But if that pleasant object is being given as a bribe to an employee of my competitor's firm in order to garner favoritism or obtain classified information, then the very same act—giving someone a pleasant object—is no longer morally justified.

In the same way, punching someone in the face because I'm a bully and don't like that person moves from being a bad act in itself to being judged morally wrong, because neither the circumstances nor my intention has changed our initial evaluation of the act. However, if a person were having a seizure, flailing his arms about, hurting others in the process, and even cutting himself on a window broken in his spasm, I might, regrettably, knock him on the jaw, rendering him unconscious. Why? In order to subdue him, protect others, and quickly secure proper medical assistance. While I'm not advocating a punch in the mouth as good medical technique, it may, in this unusual situation, be the morally right thing to do. The just-war tradition, for example, makes use of this kind of triple-font discussion in order to justify the bad acts of killing in wartime, provided the circumstances and right intention warrant the exception to the commandment "Thou shalt not kill."

Finally, shouting "Hip, Hip, Hooray" at a sporting event is a good way to show support for one's team. However, to tiptoe into a surgical operating room and shout it into the ear of the surgeon doing delicate microscopic brain surgery would be irresponsible, potentially lethal, and morally wrong. The phrase "all things being equal," used at the *act* level, is either upheld or not, depending on the *circumstances* and the *intention(s)*.

Moral decision making is not done mathematically. This triple-font model is not meant to be a rigid formula, but it does assist us in asking the right questions, in making sure that we aren't fooling ourselves, and in bringing to bear all the pertinent data when facing a moral dilemma or a complex moral issue. In question 18 we will look at some of the resources we have available to assist us in answering the triple-font questions wisely.

Q. **16. Are there any moral absolutes, actions that are always right or wrong?**

Of course there are. Worshiping God, loving one's spouse and family, and being faithful to one's commitments—these are always the right thing to do. So also, murder, rape, incest, child abuse, racism, and chauvinism—these are wrong and always remain morally unjustifiable. But some Christian scholars note that terms such as "murder" or "rape" or "child abuse" are not the names of acts purely at the *what* or "act in itself" level. "Murder" at the *what* level is an act of killing. "Rape" at the *what* level is an act of sexual intercourse. "Child abuse" at the *what* level is an act of touching. Our initial, pre-circumstances and pre-intention judgment might be that killing is bad, sex is good or at least neutral, and touching also is good or neutral. But when we add the aspect of violence to sex and touching, the manipulation and use of another person, with no self-defense justification for any of the actions, then we come to the moral conclusion that these actions are always wrong and can never be morally justified.

The terms "murder," "rape," and "child abuse" are in some sense *synthetic terms*. The triple-font process has already been done on certain acts of killing, sex, and child touching. Circumstances and intentions have already been built in. If an action fits that description, then we label it "murder," or "rape," or "child abuse," and no further circumstances or intentions will change our moral conclusion. Yes, certain actions are always right or wrong.

Q. **17. I've heard about something called "situation ethics." What is it and how does it square with our moral absolutes?**

In the 1950s and 1960s, ethicist Joseph Fletcher coined the term "situation ethics" to refer to a fairly relativistic approach to moral decision making. At one point he suggested that in each situation we should strive to do the most loving thing. That sounds a lot like what Jesus commanded, doesn't it? The difficulty is trying to discern in some complex situations what the most loving response is. For example, do I mercifully forgive my disobedient child, or should I punish the child in some way in order to help him or her learn from the mistake? Which is the more loving thing to do? As time went on, Fletcher's "situation ethics" came to be less about "love" and more about "utility," that is, calculating the greatest good for the greatest number. In each situation, one is to weigh all the consequences and to calculate the net best result, regardless of prior commitments, confidences, duties, and so on. People of personal integrity, like Martin Luther, Joan of Arc, and Thomas More, might not fare very well in Fletcher's world of "situation ethics."

Nevertheless, admitting that "situation ethics" *can* become relativistic and utilitarian does not mean that ethics or moral decision making is all theoretical. After all, our triple-font approach involves weighing circumstances and intentions, not solely judging actions in the abstract. So, in one sense, all ethics or morality really is *situational*. By that I mean that making moral decisions involves real-life situations. The eight basic questions—what, who, when, where, how, foreseeable consequences, viable alternatives, and why—are situational dimensions that are essential in evaluating a moral issue in context. In the end, Fletcher's error or bias seems to have been to focus almost exclusively on the "foreseeable consequences," whereas the Christian tradition asks all eight questions in an effort to discern wisely what is right or wrong in a given moral dilemma, situationally considered.

For example, later (QQ. 23–24) we will discuss when, if ever, it is moral to forgo potentially life-sustaining medical treatment. These bedside moral decisions always involve situational factors such as physical pain, mental suffering, financial costs, insurance benefits available—all focused on a given patient's holistic best interest. In such cases there is still an objectively right moral answer, but determining that involves weighing the pertinent circumstances of each patient in his or her unique situation. Depending on such situational factors, it may be right in one case to accept further treatment, while in another case it may be appropriate to forgo all treatment, shifting over to hospice-like care.

Q. **18. Where can we go to find help in making good moral decisions?**

The sources or resources that might be consulted to help a person make a good moral decision can be grouped under five headings: (1) scripture, (2) one's religious community and tradition, (3) the human sciences, (4) human reason or prudent reflection, and (5) prayer (i.e., making room for the Holy Spirit to work). The first three refer to sources pure and simple, while the latter two refer more to the process one should follow.

As Christians we find our fundamental faith vision and a treasury of stories, values, virtues, and case illustrations in our divinely inspired handbook, the *scriptures* or *Bible*. The seventy-two books of the Bible, particularly the twenty-seven books of the New Testament, offer us a wealth of insights into God's will, the experience and meaning of life lived in community, and challenges for Christian discipleship. As we noted above (Q. 4), the Bible is not to be read literally or too simplistically. However, with the help of some scripture commentaries, a Bible study group, and our church's ministers, we can mine the Word of God for its insights, for timeless truths to help us in our daily moral decision making. The same is true for people of other religious traditions. The Hebrew Scriptures, the Qur'an, the wisdom of Confucius, and other sacred writings offer genuine insights to peoples of various faith traditions.

In addition, we each have access to the wisdom of *our religious communities and traditions*. The Body of Christ, or the Church, with its various denominations and churches, strives to incarnate, to make real the presence and message of Jesus across time and space. Doctrinal statements and decrees, synodal and convention policies, church rules and procedures are designed to help us apply eternal gospel truths to our own time and place. Consulting one's pastor, church ministers, fellow believers, and official pronouncements is one avenue to assist us in bringing the truth of our faith tradition into dialogue with contemporary moral issues. Moral discernment is a social, not a solitary, endeavor.

The Roman Catholic church places special emphasis on its bishops and the pope, collectively known as the church's *magisterium*, as a source of theological and moral wisdom. Some ascribe to this body of leaders almost mystical powers when it comes to discerning right from wrong. Others suggest that they are blessed in a special way by God's Spirit, which empowers them for their task—to do their homework well, to consult widely, to study issues in depth, and to lead church members into a deeper communal and personal discernment process. In either instance, church members owe a special degree of respect to their church's leaders and their official decrees.

Ideally, members of every Christian denomination should seek the insights of their church's leaders, scholars, and sages as well as the sense of the faithful, or common folk wisdom. In the same way, the spirit of ecumenism and interreligious dialogue inspires us to seek truth in other Christian denominations and in the wider religious traditions of the world. In the preparation of this book, for instance, I was helped by the national offices of a number of major Christian churches, including the Evangelical Lutheran Church in America, the United Methodist Church, the Presbyterian Church U.S.A., the United Church of Christ, the United States Catholic Conference, the Southern Baptist Convention, and the Episcopal Church U.S.A. While each church treasures its own vantage point and tradition, the meaning of the mysteries of God, life, and love defies being "captured" completely by any one set of religious doctrines or any century's particular phrasing of it.

Because we are reasoning creatures, we can learn truth from our study of the *human sciences,* whether that refers to the so-called hard sciences (e.g., biology, chemistry, mathematics, economics) or the more social and aesthetic disciplines (e.g., psychology, sociology, philosophy, the arts, and theology). In order to discuss business ethics, we need to know something about how market economies work. Medical ethics requires the biological, chemical, and psychological data pertinent to a given case or issue. Each moral discussion requires competence in a given field, knowledge about the issue at hand. When it comes to making good moral decisions, ignorance is not bliss. The human sciences inform our moral discernment with essential data and insights.

Drawing on the wisdom of scripture, one's religious tradition, and the pertinent human sciences, we must finally use *our own God-given reasoning ability, both deductive and intuitive,* to make a wise or prudent decision. Like Solomon, we pray for the necessary *prudence* or *understanding heart* to reason practically, wisely, and well. Often the counsel or advice of a friend or mentor is helpful at this point. Such an advisor, as well as parents, pastors, spiritual directors, counselors, confessors, older siblings, and others in one's local faith community, may be helpful when it comes to weighing all the pros and cons of a complex moral decision.

Finally, as believers, we open this deliberation process up to *prayer, allowing God's Spirit to breathe within us,* blowing wherever the Spirit wills. We're not likely to hear specific answers from the bell tower, as Joan of Arc did, or to see visions, as Francis of Assisi did. But pausing to consciously invite God into our decision-making process does help to shift it from a merely logical exercise into true moral *discernment*. The scriptures, one's religious community and tradition, the human sciences, reason, and prayer—these remain the key sources for sound moral decision making.

Q. 19. So, can one disagree with one's church on a given moral issue and still stay a "member in good standing"?

What binds us most together, as Christians within our own churches and as Christians across denominational boundaries, is our faith in Jesus Christ, God's only son and our redeemer, who lives in and among us through the Holy Spirit. That is our core belief, which finds concise expression in our creeds, both the Apostles' Creed and the more elaborate Nicene Creed. Sadly, neither of these foundational documents spells out the Christian moral code. Yes, we are called to the virtues of faith, hope, and love, but discerning the faithful, hopeful, and loving thing to do requires further situational information. Thus, our churches have tried across the centuries to discern the parameters of Christian morality. For example, all Christian churches agree that murder, rape, adultery, and theft are wrong. Our scriptures and tradition help us determine such Christian moral norms.

However, given the situational factors mentioned above (Q. 17), not all Christian denominations come to the same conclusion about certain complex moral questions (e.g., contraception, homosexuality, capital punishment, and killing in wartime). At the same time, at various points in history, some or even all Christian churches have made mistakes, discerning incorrectly what is right or wrong. For example, as difficult as it may be for us to understand, prior to the mid-nineteenth century many Christian churches drew selectively from the writings of St. Paul in order to justify human slavery. No Christian church today would attempt to defend slavery in the name of Jesus, the prince of peace and universal love.

Thus, at any given point in history, church members must listen carefully to their denominational leaders, to consider seriously their church's official stance on a given moral question. After thoughtful, informed, and prayerful consideration, however, one is still obliged to follow one's inner conscience decision. Ideally and in most instances that will coincide with one's church's stance. But in rare cases one might feel obliged to take a stand contrary to the church's present position. In time the truth will win out, whether the church has discerned wisely and in tune with the Spirit, or whether the dissenting member is vindicated, proven to have an especially keen sense of virtue and moral rightness.

Through it all there should be a spirit of mutual respect and charity. Some churches, mostly in the Protestant family and especially those governed more congregationally, place a strong emphasis on the freedom of each local community and each individual Christian to discern his or her own response where consensus is lacking. Other churches, particularly the Roman Catholic and Orthodox communities, place greater emphasis on community solidarity, recommending that "when in doubt," a church member ought to side with that denomination's official moral position. These churches believe that members ought to presume in favor of their official teachings. Only in the gravest of moral issues (e.g., blatant racism, bigotry, or licentiousness), where public scandal is a distinct possibility, might a church take action to dismiss or "excommunicate" a member who sincerely struggles with moral doubts or disagreement. Dialogue rather than dismissal, mutual respect rather than denunciation ought to be the earmarks of Christians who disagree about a controversial moral issue.

Q. **20. How would you summarize the Christian approach to morality and moral decision making?**

I would go directly to the Gospels of Matthew, Mark, and Luke, to the passage in which Jesus is asked, "Which commandment is the first of all?" (Mark 12:28–34; Matt. 22:34–40; Luke 10:25–38). You might be thinking only of the Ten Commandments, but in fact there are 613 commandments in the Old Testament law. This question was a common brainteaser, asked of well-known teachers and rabbis. If you had to drop 612 commandments and keep only one, which would you choose? It is as if Jesus answered that he couldn't sum everything up in only one commandment, but if they would let him have two, he could encompass the Law and the Prophets, the meaning of life itself.

First, he chose the Jewish prayer known as the *Shema:* "Hear, O Israel: the Lord our God, the Lord is one; you shall love the Lord your God with all your heart, and with all your soul, and with all your mind, and with all your strength" (Deut. 6:4). Devout Jews begin all their daily prayers with this affirmation. To this pledge of fidelity to God, Jesus added the second commandment: "You shall love your neighbor as yourself" (Lev. 19:18). By linking these together—*love* of God, neighbor, and self—Jesus has given us a succinct summary of Christian morality.

Love is not synonymous with constant pleasure or fun. Genuine love is a difficult and multifaceted reality. It involves some measure of self-fulfillment. Likewise, love entails some experience of mutuality or friendship. But true love, lasting or abiding love, fundamentally involves self-giving and sacrifice, a willingness to "go the extra mile," to "turn the other cheek," and to be there for the other, "in good times *and in bad*," over the long haul. The rest of this book, the eighty questions and responses that follow, will be a humble attempt to enflesh Jesus' love commandment as we strive to live it out in various moral arenas. Faithful and committed love—for God, neighbor, and self—is the earmark of Christian morality, indeed the basis and benchmark for all human morality.

PART TWO————————————————————————————

Issues in Healthcare Ethics

Q. 21. What do you mean by "healthcare ethics"? What does Christianity have to say about morality and healthcare?

Sometimes people use the term "bioethics." Others prefer "medical ethics" or even "biomedical ethics." While there may be a shade of scholarly difference between these various terms, in general they all refer to the same thing—the moral issues surrounding health, sickness, medical treatment, and medical research. In some sense *healthcare ethics* dates back at least to Greece in the fifth century before Christ. A young physician named Hippocrates crafted an oath, a profession of faith and morality, which he pledged before the gods. In a sacred covenant, he swore to be true to his mentor, who had taught him the healing arts, to his mentor's family, *and to those patients who would come under his care.*

What did he promise? Hippocrates vowed to use his medical skills solely to benefit the sick, or at least to cause them no undue harm. He would give no deadly drug nor suggest it to a patient (i.e., euthanasia). He refused to perform abortions. Hippocrates pledged to respect the integrity of his patients (1) by causing them no injustice, (2) by not making sexual advances to patients (be they male or female, slave or free), and (3) by keeping confidential the information learned within the privileged doctor–patient relationship. While most physicians, nurses, and healthcare professionals today do not take the Hippocratic oath, they do subscribe to similar codes of ethical conduct, often inscribed in the charters of various professional organizations and societies (e.g., American Medical Association, American Nurses Association).

If one were to look for the roots of healthcare morality in the scriptures, one need only go to the first chapter of the book of Genesis to find our core value or principle:

> So God created humankind in his image, in the image of God he created them; male and female he created them. God blessed them, and God said to them, "Be fruitful and multiply, and fill the earth and subdue it"; . . . God saw everything that he had made, and indeed, it was very good. (Gen 1:27–28, 31)

Every human life is inherently valuable and worthy of respect, not because a human has earned respect or deserves it but simply because God says so. Each person is made in the image of God. Despite our differences in intelligence, strength, and talents, and despite our tendency to make mistakes, to sin, and not to "measure up," we still bear the imprint of the Creator's divine touch, the breath of life itself. The story of Genesis goes on to suggest that disease and death are somehow mysteriously bound up with the dark side of life, with the powers of evil and sin. Against the backdrop of our physical fragility and our human tendency toward unhealthy, often sinful choices, the Hebrew Scriptures constantly reflect our need for God's healing and mercy.

In the Gospels we find Jesus applying the image of the physician to himself. "Those who are well have no need of a physician, but those who are sick; I have come to call not the righteous but sinners" (Mark 2:17; Luke 5:31–32; Matt. 9:12). Again and again he brings healing to those infirmed in body as well as in spirit—the blind, the deaf, the mute, the lame, lepers, those possessed by demons, and even the dead. "I came that they may have life and have it abundantly," he proclaims (John 10:10). In the story of the good Samaritan, Jesus points out that it is in binding up our brother's [or sister's] wounds, in caring for those who are hurt or in need, that we too assist in bringing about God's reign here on earth (Luke 10:29–37).

That is not to say that death is the ultimate enemy, nor that it is to be forestalled at all costs. Christians value life in its *totality*. We are alive physically, yes, but also mentally, socially, and spiritually. We believe in eternal life, a life beyond disease, death, and the grave. But while we live on earth, we are entrusted as stewards of this phase of life, commanded to foster health, growth, and human well-being, for ourselves and others.

Across the centuries, Christian believers have taken seriously this challenge to respect life and to foster healing. A vast network of hospitals, nursing homes, clinics, and other healthcare ministries gives evidence of our commitment to the healing arts. But it is primarily in the last five hundred years, since the beginning of modern medicine—surgery, anesthesia, hygiene, microbiology, and pharmacology—that the formal study of healthcare morality has emerged. And again, in the mid to late twentieth century there has been a burgeoning of advances in medical technology, accompanied by a renewed interest in medicine and healthcare ethics.

Q. **22. Does every person have a right to good health? And, if so, why is there so much illness and suffering?**

No, people have no inalienable right to expect good health any more than they can expect to be born with "good looks," intelligence, musical talent, or any other blessing to the good, better, or best degree. All things being equal, we are born with a modicum of good health—all our appendages and inner organs in place, all our faculties and senses operative. But even then, some people are born visually impaired, hearing deficient, or physically disabled. Down through the ages people have asked why a good God allows such afflictions as genetic diseases, birth defects, or the ravages of a mother's drug addiction or AIDS on newborns. No one can adequately answer why some people get cancer, heart disease, or other infringements on good health.

At times we can point to our own behavior—poor eating habits, a lack of exercise, smoking, and the like—but often the causes of disease are mysterious. So too the aging process. Why? Earthly life—physical life as we know it—is a transitory thing, and there are no guarantees of a perfect body or of perfect health across our life span. But we do have a basic duty to safeguard our own good health, and, in that, we have a right to access society's healthcare resources. Whether we pay for it by the sweat of our brow (i.e., insurance, personal expenditures) or seek access as a matter of social justice (i.e., Medicare, Medicaid, welfare programs), one has a "right" to care and human services, not the promise of a cure or a guarantee that treatment will be effective. "Health" is an elusive thing, a fleeting blessing. Sickness and disease are a part of the human condition. Ultimately medicine, even high-tech, state-of-the-art medicine, falls short. Death comes to us all.

Q. **23. Do we have to do everything to fight death? Is it ever right to say, "Halt—stop all the machines—I've had enough"?**

Each of us has the moral right to seek ongoing medical treatment, if it offers us some reasonable hope of benefit and can be obtained without excessive burden or expense. Likewise, we have an equal right to refuse any and all treatment, if, on balance, it offers little or no hope of benefit or if it entails grave burden or cost. This is not a particularly liberal moral position, but is the standard Christian formula, dating back at least to the 1500s. You may have heard it called "ordinary" versus "extraordinary" means. Some today are calling it "proportionate" versus "disproportionate" treatment.

The key is in balancing or weighing *benefits* and *burdens* from the patient's perspective. If the benefits of further medical treatment outweigh the burdens, then "ordinarily" one would be expected to accept such treatment. If you will be more helped than hurt by accepting a proposed medical treatment, it is logical to seek such help. We are stewards of our lives, entrusted to preserve life wherever reasonable healing is possible. However, if the burdens associated with treatment outweigh the benefits—even if that benefit is staying alive itself—then it would be "extraordinary" to expect a person to accept this therapy. Why overburden yourself for too little benefit? That would be a kind of self-imposed torture.

What constitutes a benefit or a burden? First of all, will the treatment save my life? For how long? At what cost? At what level of physical and mental function? How much pain or broader suffering is involved? What will be the effect on my family, my loved ones, and my community? In the 1950s Pope Pius XII spoke about the right of patients to determine their own course of treatment based on an assessment of reasonable hope of benefit versus grave or excessive burdens. One ought not to give up the fight for life and improved health prematurely. But neither is one obliged to stay alive at all costs, whether physical, psychological, social, or spiritual. In question 21 we proposed that human life is our fundamental value, but the *totality* of life is not summed up in prolonged respiration and circulation. Each person has the right and responsibility to make his or her own determination concerning medical treatment at the edges of life.

Q. **24. But that sounds like "situation ethics." What might be beneficial to you may not be beneficial enough to me. Is the ordinary/extraordinary-means tradition a form of relativism?**

No, but it does require situational information before a morally right or objective judgment can be made. Two people with an identical cancer or disease might really have differences in weighing benefits and burdens. To one person, staying alive at almost all costs might seem desirable. His daughter's wedding is coming up soon and it is his deepest desire to be there, to walk her down the aisle. The other cancer patient is single and has completed all his personal and financial dealings. He has bid farewell to his loved ones and has no major reason to accept a largely experimental, costly, and minimally effective round of chemotherapy. In addition, the father of the bride has a high tolerance for pain, has experienced few side effects from previous chemotherapy, and is well insured. Our single patient has a low tolerance for pain, is terribly afraid of hospitals, has experienced both hair loss and severe nausea during prior chemotherapy, and is nearing the end of his insurance limits.

For the former patient, one might objectively say that the benefit of this risky chemotherapy outweighs the burden. For him it is "ordinary" and he ought to say yes. For the latter patient the burdens seem to outweigh the minimal potential for benefit. One might objectively say that for him the proposed therapy is "extraordinary," optional, even contraindicated. He probably ought to say no. Relativism? Not at all. This is an objective moral judgment based on real situational factors, focused on each individual as a unique person.

Q. **25. What about writing a "living will"? Are these morally acceptable? Should a person write one as he or she grows older?**

In recent years there has been a lot of discussion about *advance directives*, the technical term for documents that are commonly known as "living wills." According to the Christian tradition as well as federal law, a competent adult patient has the right to be the primary decision-maker concerning any and all medical treatment. As we discussed above, only you can decide whether a given treatment will be more beneficial or burdensome to you, given your life, your tolerance for pain, your finances, your values, and your prioritizing of those values. But what if someone becomes incapacitated by accident, stroke, Alzheimer's disease, or permanent coma? How do we, as a community, still respect that person's right to say "forge ahead" or "halt"? Advance directives are a helpful tool, a legal means to guarantee that one's wishes will be respected and carried out.

There are three types of advance directives. The first, the one most commonly called a *living will*, is a document in which you attempt to define situations in which you would want further treatment and situations in which you would prefer that all such efforts cease, shifting over to a mandate for nursing and hospice-like care only. Such living wills vary from simple, one-paragraph documents to elaborate checklists of diseases and therapy options.

The second kind of advance directive, a *durable power of attorney for healthcare,* involves designating another person to serve as your substitute or proxy decision-maker, should the need ever arise. By granting this proxy power to some family member or trusted friend, you are asking all others—family, friends, your physician, the hospital or institution, and even the wider society—to accept your designated proxy's decision as if it were your own. Your proxy is free to hear all the pertinent facts of the case, to weigh all treatment options, and to make a decision based as much as possible on the values he or she knows that you hold dear. Many think this is the clearest moral and legal option.

The third option is a *combination document*, blending the previous two into one. One would give durable power of attorney for healthcare to a proxy, while in the same document offering one's living will instructions concerning one's views of life, death, health, faith, and forgoing treatment in general.

Yes, all three types of advance directives are considered moral, legal, and even useful tools in a society that wants to respect moral values and choices about medical actions should one ever become unable to speak for oneself. Provided one does not request assistance in committing suicide (i.e., euthanasia), there is no moral problem with having an advance directive. While there is no moral obligation to write such a document, families, physicians, hospitals, and lawcourts often are grateful if a patient who becomes incompetent has expressed his or her wishes in writing. If you opt to write an advance directive, *now* is the time. These are not solely or even primarily a tool for senior citizens. Karen Ann Quinlan and Nancy Cruzan, whose famous cases dragged on in the courts and in the media, were each in their twenties when tragedy struck. So, senior citizens, middle-aged people, and young adults would all do well to craft a living will, to designate in writing a healthcare proxy, or to create a combination of the two.

In most states one does not need to hire an attorney to draft such a document. Have it witnessed, notarized, and distributed to the appropriate people—physician, family, close friends, and your attorney. If and when the time comes for others to make a decision on your behalf, you will be there "in spirit" with your advance directive. All will rest easier knowing that they tried to carry out your conscience, your wishes, your "living will."

Q. **26. What does Christianity say about suicide, euthanasia, and physician-assisted suicide?**

Our basic and abiding respect for the dignity of every human person leads us to put a moral fence around human life, either forbidding all human killing (absolute pacifism) or else hemming in the few exceptions with as many restrictions as possible. Across the centuries most Christians have not interpreted the commandment "Thou shalt not kill" in a cut-and-dried or literal sense. Killing an unjust aggressor in self-defense, killing enemy soldiers in the case of a "just war" (see Q. 82), and even executing criminals (see QQ. 88–89) have been some of the exceptions to the general prohibition of taking human life. However, it has generally been accepted by most Christians, indeed by the wider society as well, that there ought to be a prohibition against killing *innocent* persons. Thus, there has been a long-standing moral prohibition of suicide or assisted suicide, even in the case of those suffering from debilitating or terminal illness.

Christians generally have interpreted a patient's desire for death in such extreme situations to be more a cry for help, for care, and for comfort than a clearly rational desire for assistance in committing suicide. The hospice movement, pastoral ministry to patients and their families, and specialized pain-management therapies are all designed to accompany someone into and through the dying process as humanely as possible. To most Christians and Christian churches this commitment to care for the dying seems preferable to stepping on the slippery slope of euthanasia, killing innocent people because they request it or because they or we "mean well" by our killing efforts.

At one point in church history pastors were encouraged to refuse Christian burial for someone who had committed suicide. Fortunately, in recent decades that pastorally insensitive approach has been abandoned. It is assumed that in most instances the person who commits suicide is suffering from severe depression and therefore *subjectively* is not culpable for their *objectively* wrong decision. Christian burial is offered in part to comfort the surviving family members and in part prayerfully to send the deceased on his or her way to God, who is love, full of mercy and compassion.

Obviously, there are others, some in our churches and more in the wider society (e.g., the Hemlock Society, Derek Humphry, Dr. Jack Kevorkian) who disagree with this interpretation. They believe firmly that terminally ill persons who wish to kill themselves are morally justified and ought to be allowed legally to seek the direct assistance of a physician or others. Presently we are at a major crossroad in legal and moral discussions about what ought and ought not to be done to ease the suffering of dying patients.

If one believes that the prohibition against killing the innocent is absolute, as do Catholics and many evangelicals, then assisted suicide or euthanasia is out of the question. However, there are other mainline Christians who might accept the possible morality of assisted suicide in theory, but who foresee too many negative consequences if it were to become a societally accepted practice. Would it remain voluntary or would persons who opt for longer, arguably futile courses of treatment be coerced into accepting the lethal step? Would insurance companies be open to financing more expensive alternatives to the "quick fix" of euthanasia? What about cases involving incompetent or comatose patients? Would the life-respecting nature of the doctor–patient relationship be harmed if killing became a possible "therapy"?

In short, the debate about assisted suicide or euthanasia raises a red flag for most Christian churches, whether more liberal or more conservative in their moral bases. Crossing the heretofore absolute prohibition against killing "innocent people" has broad moral ramifications not only for the individuals involved but for all of us as a community as well. With deep compassion and empathy for those who are suffering and for those who linger long, it seems that hospice care and a ministry to accompany people through their natural dying process are morally preferable to suicide or societally assisted euthanasia.

Q. 27. Then how is refusing extraordinarily burdensome or disproportionate means any different from assisted suicide?

There is a fine line of difference, but an important one, between refusing disproportionate means, allowing a patient to die a natural death, and choosing to kill a patient. In the classic ordinary/ extraordinary-means tradition the focus is on the value of a given treatment option for this patient in his or her unique situation. Whether death can be foreseen as imminent or not, the patient (or one's family) tries to weigh whether the benefits of doing this treatment outweigh the burdens. That is not the same as saying, "Will refusal of this treatment or removal of this machine get me (or my loved one) dead?" Rather, the decision is whether my life, on balance, will be more helped or hurt by accepting this therapy, regardless of whether I remain alive or may die soon after it is administered.

Thus, in 1975 the Quinlan family had to judge whether, on balance, their comatose daughter Karen Ann was being more helped or hurt by having a ventilator force her lungs to breathe. She was not brain dead, but all indications were that her brain was so nearly dead that she could not and would never be able to breathe on her own again. Her parents, with the support of their Catholic pastor and local bishop, requested that the ventilator be removed. They believed that it served more to prolong her natural dying process than to offer her any hope of recovery. Ironically, although everyone anticipated that she would die soon after the artificial life-support was removed, Karen began to breathe on her own. Her lower brain or stem function was more viable than all had thought. With the help of a nursing home, her parents continued to care for her over the next decade until she died a natural death.

It would seem that their decision to remove the ventilator was not an attempt to kill Karen Ann but a judgment made about the relative benefit to her of continued ventilator dependence. If she had died, would they have been surprised? No, they were probably hoping, maybe even praying, that God would take her home. But they did not look for the next thing to remove or propose injecting their daughter with lethal drugs; they cared for her lovingly over the remaining years of her life. Thus, the decision to forgo or remove a therapy judged too burdensome or of too little benefit is not the same as a decision to kill the patient.

 28. What about pain medications? I've heard that it is morally permissible to administer even lethal doses of pain medications and that this is not considered euthanasia. I don't understand this.

As you phrase it, I would be confused too. Willfully to administer lethal doses of morphine or any other painkiller, with the explicit intention of killing the patient, is clearly assisted suicide or euthanasia. However benignly intended by the perpetrator, it is immoral and unlawful, punishable in most states under homicide statutes. There have been well publicized cases in which a nursing home employee took it upon herself or himself to inject elderly patients with an intentionally lethal dose of some painkilling chemical. Even if such questionable "angels of mercy" mean well (subjective culpability), their behavior cannot be excused in the objective moral and legal arenas.

That said, it has been a long-standing part of mainline Christian healthcare that terminally ill patients should be made as comfortable as possible. Some choose to forgo potentially addictive painkillers either because they fear becoming substance-dependent or because they would rather live with a bit more pain if it means they will be more conscious, more aware of their surroundings and loved ones in attendance. Others, because of the excruciating pain of their condition (e.g., bone cancer) and with little fear of addiction in their dying days, prefer to be "doped up," kept as pain-free as modern pharmaceuticals will allow. Sufficient dosages depend on a variety of factors—a patient's body size, pain tolerance, kind of pain, location of pain, effectiveness of other comfort measures, etc. Therefore, there is no neat chart that gives exact dosages. So too, one can become immune to certain painkillers or to lower dosages as time passes.

Many Christian ethicists and churches accept the principle that one may give incremental doses of morphine, or other painkillers, up to and including borderline lethal doses, provided that killing the patient is *not* one's intention and that such borderline lethal levels were arrived at by small, medically indicated increments over a reasonable therapeutic time frame. In short, at some point the levels of painkiller may, indirectly and unintentionally, also be having an impact on the shallowness of the now-dying patient's breathing. As long as it is not our intention to suffocate this patient, we can tolerate this borderline risk in our direct and intended effort to keep excruciating pain at bay. This is standard Catholic and mainline Protestant morality. It is the practice in many hospices and hospitals. However, some healthcare professionals and some more fundamentalistic Christian churches are squeamish about this, fearing that this borders on indirect euthanasia.

The key issue seems to be that of intention. If one intends to kill the patient by these injections, then it is a species of euthanasia, albeit subtly and somewhat indirectly caused. If, however, one is focusing on pain management and not on terminating the patient's life, such incremental injections can be seen as beneficial, not intentionally lethal. They are acceptable, with the possible impact on already shallow breathing being secondary, indirect, and unintended.

Q. **29. One last treatment question—what about artificial tube feeding and fluids? Is it ever moral to "starve" someone to death?**

This is currently the "cutting-edge" issue in many healthcare ethics conferences and seminars. First of all, it is important to note that no major Christian body suggests that all dying patients should be force-fed or hooked up to artificial feeding apparatuses. Since at least the 1500s it has been standard practice to offer dying patients fluids and nourishment by mouth, as often and as much as they want, but not to force them to ingest their proper caloric or nutritional intake. Comfort seems to take precedence over proper nutrition in the case of patients near death. Some suggest that this falls under the burden-versus-benefit umbrella of the ordinary/extraordinary-means tradition. The relative benefit to a dying patient of receiving full and proper nutrition may be outweighed by the fact that it will prolong life very little and may be too burdensome to administer, given one's level of pain or consciousness. In these terminal cases we do not mandate intravenous feeding, naso-gastric tubes, or gastrostomies (stomach tubes) to ensure proper nutrition and hydration.

The real controversy about artificially administered fluids and nutrition centers on patients who are permanently unconscious, whether in a comatose state (eyes never open) or what is called permanent vegetative state (eyes may be open, closed, or vary, but patient remains "unconscious"). One school of thought asserts that feeding someone through a naso-gastric tube, an intravenous line, or directly through a tube into the stomach must be weighed, like any other medical treatment, in terms of its benefit as well as its burdens for the patient, holistically considered. If one is permanently unconscious—provided sufficient time and tests have occurred to ensure that one's condition is truly irreversible—then it is arguable that long-term force-feeding is too burdensome and too costly for the benefit of sustaining mere respiration and circulation, the physical aspects of life. It is argued that respect for life means respect for human life in its totality—physical, mental, social, and spiritual dimensions. If all potential for mental and social life has ceased for this patient, and if his or her spiritual and eternal life is being stalled at death's door, then prolonging the physiological aspects of life by artificial and costly means is not a sufficient benefit, given the patient's totality or holistic best interest.

Another school of thought suggests that food and water ought to be seen not as medical treatment but as part of basic humane nursing care, at least in the case of permanently unconscious patients. Those who hold this view believe that, in the vast majority of cases, administering hydration and nutrition, even by artificial means, is "ordinary" and therefore obligatory care, of sufficient benefit regardless of burden. The debate seems to center on whether remaining alive at the level of permanent unconsciousness is of benefit *to the patient* or not. Some will argue that the patient is of benefit to the rest of us, that keeping him or her alive bespeaks our respect for life, even the lives of our most tragic and unproductive members. By keeping such patients alive we attest to all those with disabilities that we care about them in a divine way, not based on their functional potential, but rather highlighting their inherent dignity as human beings. The difficulty with this well-intended defense is that we are now not weighing burden and benefit *to the patient*, but we have turned such patients into objects of our care, the main beneficiaries being we and our community.

So what is the official Christian conclusion? We don't have one. Church leaders, ethicists, and healthcare practitioners sincerely line up on both sides of the question of artificially administered fluid and nutrition. Archbishop John Roach, of the Catholic archdiocese of St. Paul, Minnesota, summed up the position of mainline Christians on this issue:

> Both of these options accept the inviolability of human life and the obligation to sustain life by suitable means. Both attempt to apply these principles conscientiously to a difficult case. The Bio/medical Ethics Commission believes that it is morally permissible to act on the basis of either of these opinions at the present time. The withdrawal of the feeding tube from a permanently unconscious patient may plausibly be viewed as the withdrawal of disproportionate or extraordinary means. (*The Catholic Bulletin,* 7 March 1991)

Q.
30. Another hot topic in medical ethics is abortion. Why don't the Christian churches agree on the moral question of abortion?

Why various Christian bodies disagree about the morality of abortion is best understood if we first look at the basic moral questions surrounding abortion. There is no doubt that a human embryo en route to becoming a fetus en route to being born an infant is both a member of the human species and "innocent." She or he didn't ask to be conceived. Nor did she or he have any control over that decision. All things being equal, it would seem that the prohibition against killing the innocent would cover the pre-born human life as well, making abortion an immoral action. Most Christians and Christian communities accept this as their basic starting point. Terminating human life *in utero* is not a neutral act. But the difficulty is the phrase "all things being equal." Some Christian bodies, most notably Catholics and Baptists, believe that the prohibition against abortion is practically absolute. Even if the mother's life is threatened by the pregnancy or if the fetus has been conceived through an act of rape or violent incest, the fetus remains "innocent" and his or her life cannot be forfeited.

Other mainline Christians and their churches prohibit most abortions, certainly those of convenience or when abortion is one's chosen method of birth control. But in the case of rape, forced incest, or if the mother's very life or basic health is at risk, then "all things are not equal." According to some Christian churches, these may be the exceptional situations in which abortion tragically may be the lesser of two evils and may thus be morally justified, albeit with regret. One also must add to these "conflict" situations the ongoing debate about the status and rights of an embryo or fetus, especially when the mother's life or health is at risk.

Is the fetus a *person*? Does the fetus have an *immortal soul*? When does an embryo/fetus become a human person, an ensouled individual, with all the abiding dignity and rights ascribed to full members of our human community? At the moment of conception? After implantation in the uterus as twins, triplets, or one individual? About forty days after conception, when brain waves begin? When it is able to live outside the womb (about twenty to twenty-four weeks)?

At birth? Surely from the moment of conception we have the human genome, the genetic map that will develop into a full human person. Is that sufficient to declare him or her a person? Does the zygote have an unconditional right to life, to come to full-term birth? "All things being equal," most Christians would defend that zygote's right to become an embryo, a fetus, and a full-term baby.

Therefore, most Christians believe that the vast majority of the 1.5 million abortions performed in the United States each year are wrong, objectively immoral choices. One could say that all life issues are or ought to be linked, viewed in relation to each other, like "a seamless garment." Pope John Paul II's encyclical *The Gospel of Life* calls all people to respect, protect, love, and serve human life from the womb to the tomb.

Q. **31. But you seemed to leave a loophole open by saying "all things being equal." Are some abortions moral, even if most are not?**

The Catholic tradition, with others concurring, says that no *direct* abortion is ever moral. If one does the deed by direct means (suction, D & C, saline solution, etc.) or if one intends that an abortion occur, even if one's actions only indirectly cause it, then that person is guilty of a *direct* abortion. However, in rare instances, where an abortion may occur indirectly and unintended, one may knowingly permit or allow such *indirect* abortions to occur, regrettably so. For instance? If a woman has a cancerous uterus and is also six to eight weeks pregnant, one may legitimately remove the cancerous organ (i.e., hysterectomy) to save her life, knowing that the now-nonviable fetus will be removed at the same time. If one could wait until the fetus comes to full term or could transfer it to a surrogate mother or artificial womb, one most likely would do so. But in this tragic situation, all things are *not* equal, and accepting the indirect and undesired loss of the fetus is morally tolerable.

One might also make a similar case in terms of an ectopic pregnancy, though not all agree that this fits the traditional moral distinction between bad acts directly intended and those indirectly caused but not intended. These rare instances are the only exceptions that the Catholic tradition makes to the categorical prohibition of all abortions. Abortion is seen as one of the most serious of moral choices because it is about a human life and that pre-born life is the most innocent and vulnerable of all.

As noted above, there are some Christians who would expand the "exceptions" list to include some few *direct* abortions, but only in the extreme cases where either the mother's life or health is endangered or, perhaps, where she is as innocent as the fetus, the conception being the result of rape or violent incest. These constitute about 3 percent of the abortions in this country. Some Christians are willing to allow these to be reserved or set aside in anti-abortion laws, as the rare, possibly debatable exceptions to the rule that, *all things being equal,* abortion is immoral.

Beyond this, there are some, including a few Protestant churches, who defend the termination of pregnancy if the fetus is severely deformed, with various definitions of "severely" being set forth. Others suggest that because of societal chauvinism, because of the male patriarchy that dominates both our society and our legal system, a woman ought to have the right to decide for herself whether to abort or not. This view, however, hinges on the status ascribed to pre-born life. If the embryo or fetus in question is considered a human person, as many Christians hold, then the mother would have no personal right to terminate its life. Fetal status bumps up against the rightful respect due women in our society. In all cases of abortion, we must be mindful of the objective/subjective distinction noted earlier (QQ. 13–14). A woman's subjective responsibility or guilt must be judged with sensitivity and compassion, even if one has strong feelings about the objective immorality of the act of abortion itself. The rhetoric of the pro-life movement and the pro-choice movement, each with both thoughtful and fringe proponents, makes this a very delicate and difficult subject.

Q. **32. What do you think about those anti-abortion demonstrators who kill abortion doctors and declare that it is a moral solution?**

I find such tactics tragic, misguided, and immoral. Those who defend such actions either see them as a matter of raw numbers (e.g., two doctors dead versus 1.5 million fetuses) or else they argue self-defense or justifiable killing, as in a war. Certainly the Christian tradition surrounding legitimate *conscientious objection* allows that one might break an immoral civil law, if by so doing one draws public attention to the injustice, in the hope of effecting a change in public sentiment and law. Thus, chaining oneself to a fence or trespassing on private property might be acceptable symbolic actions—illegal but not necessarily immoral in the larger scheme of things. However, if the harm done is immoral, reprehensible, or of a similar nature to that which one is protesting, then it is very questionable whether one is committing an act of true "civil disobedience." Is he or she not committing an immoral and illegal offense similar to the one being protested?

It is doubtful that killing obstetricians or gynecologists who perform abortions will somehow stop many abortions or lead to a change in the legality of abortions. Those who kill these physicians may be subjectively sincere, but that in no way makes their actions objectively right or legally tenable. Impacting or changing the societal acceptance of abortion as a "private action" or a "legal right" is more complex than shooting abortion doctors one at a time. The old adage "two wrongs don't make a right" seems applicable here.

More importantly, I have serious qualms about persons who are adamantly opposed to one kind of killing (i.e., abortion), but who are enthusiastic proponents of other killing, whether that be the execution of abortion doctors, military actions in general, or capital punishment. Those who advocate a *seamless-garment* approach to pro-life issues, those who challenge us to be consistent in our defense of life, seem to me to be closer to the gospel message of Jesus than those who pick and choose their life concerns. That does not mean that being anti-abortion automatically makes one anti–capital punishment, or anti-war in all instances. But being pro-life in the broader or fuller sense should give one pause in any moral question that impacts human life. Our ethical approach concerning life questions should be holistic, a seamless garment. Therefore, those who advocate violence against pro-choice advocates are not truly pro-life, but merely anti-abortion. That is not consistent with the gospel of life, the call to respect life—human life, animal and plant life, indeed all of God's creation.

Q. **33. On my driver's license there is a space to check if I want to be an organ donor. What does the Christian tradition have to say about organ transplants? Is it moral to be an organ donor?**

Ever since Mary Shelley frightened us with her tales of Dr. Frankenstein's monster, we seem to be both fascinated and repelled by the thought of transplanting body parts from one person to another. In a very real sense blood transfusions, which have been an accepted part of medical practice for over a century, are a form of transplant. So too skin, kidneys, livers, eye parts, pancreatic tissue, bone marrow, and even human hearts are all transplantable. The basic moral question is whether to give or to receive an organ for transplant is morally right, Christian, and humane.

With the exception of Jehovah's Witnesses, who are well known for their prohibition against "drinking blood"(transfusions), most mainline Christian groups commend the generosity of those who voluntarily donate organs at the time of death or who are willing to be live donors, where such a donation does not pose undue risk to the donor. The Red Cross and other agencies rely on the charity and civic-mindedness of people to keep blood banks reasonably well stocked. So too, major transplant centers frequently mount public-relations campaigns to encourage people to sign organ donor cards. There are also sophisticated screening programs that seek live donors voluntarily to share a kidney, bone marrow, or other replenishable tissue, either for a blood relative in need or for a stranger with a reasonably close genetic match.

Some suggest that a living donor is morally justified in giving away a kidney or bone marrow or at least in giving blood under the principle of *totality*. That is, the donor's holistic well-being or sense of self is enhanced by his or her magnanimous gift of a vital body part to someone in need. Others argue that one can't stretch the meaning of one person's totality or best interest to include organs ending up inside someone else. Totality proponents counter that "respect for life" means life in its fullness, not solely the physical aspects of life. Being an organ donor might enhance one's psychological well-being, one's social sense of camaraderie with the recipient, and even one's spiritual sense of duty or charity, all of which accrue as great benefit for relatively little risk or burden. Others sidestep the "totality" debate altogether and merely say that donating an organ is charitable, loving, Christian, and humane.

Recently, some controversy has arisen about "when" one may remove organs from a dying patient. The tragic situation of anencephalic infants, who have no upper brain at all, is a case in point. It might seem useful or even practical to remove organs from such patients while they are still alive, while those organs are being sustained by oxygen and blood flow. However, that patient is not yet deceased and deserves our respect through his or her natural dying process. Removing organs before death, especially vital organs (i.e., the heart), can become the actual cause of death. From a Christian perspective it is inappropriate to "kill" a patient, even one near death, in order to recover his or her organs for others. In this instance, a practical desire to help others by using the organs at hand comes into conflict with the abiding respect for the human dignity and dying process of the patient. The dying patient's dignity ought to take precedence, even if some transplantable organs deteriorate and are lost in the process.

 34. What about organ recipients? Can wealthy people buy cadaver or live donor organs? What about all those pitiful children spotlighted on talk shows and in magazines? Who gets whose organs?

These questions all are focused on the justice and equity of organ distribution. Since there are currently too few organs for those in need, a national registry system has been created. Ideally it is meant both to facilitate a broader, nationwide search for good tissue matches and to foster greater fairness in determining who gets the next available organ for transplant. If one passes initial medical screening, one's name is added to the list of candidates for transplant. After that, decisions are made based on tissue match, severity of one's condition, potential for a positive outcome, and length of time on the waiting list. This seems to be the most fair way to assure that all have access to a scarce social resource.

One exception to this "first come, first served" approach to distribution is the donation of tissue or organs within one's own family network. Blood relatives often make better tissue matches. Moreover, there is a family bond that the wider community respects and even promotes. A parent sacrificing a kidney for a child or siblings willing to undergo bone marrow transplants for one another—these are the soul and sinew of family love and sacrifice. Organ designation is moral and commendable in such instances. Still, it is important that such donations be voluntary, not coerced by family pressure or guilt.

There is greater concern, however, when a given family goes public in seeking an organ for their loved one from an anonymous "Good Samaritan." At first glance, making a personal plea through talk shows or newspapers seems to be a bold and caring venture. Surely those who expend such energy are doing so because they love their ailing relative. In other words, their intention is sincere. But, as we've noted before, "meaning well" is not the sole measure of right and wrong. I would suggest that it is unfair for one family—with more money, with more political clout, with greater access to media outlets, with more personality or photogenic charisma—to circumvent the universal registry system. Fair is fair and there is already a societally accepted procedure for applying for access to transplant services and waiting one's turn for the next available organ. It's not a perfect system. At times the wealthy or powerful do "beat the system," but such favoritism seems unjust, immoral, and a disservice to those dutifully waiting their rightful turn.

Other moral questions focus on whether we ought to keep organ donation in the voluntary "gift" arena, or whether we ought to "presume consent," allowing for routine removal of organs from those newly dead. A mid-course, adopted in some state statutes, is to mandate that a request be made of all families when a loved one is near death or has been killed. Ghoulish as this may sound, it seems to be a reasonable moral middle ground between taking organs without consent or relying on purely voluntary donations. The commercialization of organs is another moral concern, though in most instances state and federal laws prohibit the buying and selling of nonreplenishable body parts. Should national boundaries be upheld, or do other countries have a right to access our advanced organ transplant technology? Who, if anyone, may consent for live donation from incompetent persons—fetuses, infants, children, mentally disabled or comatose persons?

Finally, if one's vital organs stop functioning, especially if more than one system fails, should we so facilely expect replacement surgery? It is at least worth asking whether the shutdown of one's vital organ systems is not an indication that a person is "dying." Should transplants become the wave of the future, or would we be better to focus on better care for the dying? It is not heartless to ask. Nor is there one obvious moral or Christian answer. Organ transplants are a cutting-edge therapy to which many commit their lives, their talents, and their very organs. The moral questions are many. Churches have not sought to resolve prematurely all the related moral questions. This is an ongoing debate, with much good will but few ready answers.

Q. **35. Speaking of cutting-edge medical issues, what about genetic screening and genetic engineering?**

This is a timely question, especially considering the Human Genome Project now under way. In 1991 the United States Congress authorized funds for a massive, fifteen-year research program to map the entire human genetic package. Most of us have heard of chromosomes, genes, and DNA. But few of us realize how complex the human genome map really is. The twenty-three chromosome pairs that we may have studied in high school biology class actually mushroom into between seventy-five and one hundred thousand distinct structural genes. Already scientists have discovered the location of the genes that cause cystic fibrosis, diabetes, hemophilia, sickle cell anemia, Down's Syndrome, muscular dystrophy, Alzheimer's disease and Huntington's disease. In most cases therapeutic use of this information is still a long way off, but knowing the location of the genetic defect is an essential first step to understanding these conditions.

Moral questions seem to focus on two areas, *genetic screening* and potential *gene therapies*. In terms of genetic screening, there are two kinds: (1) *prenatal screening of fetuses* to determine if they have any major genetic diseases or deformities and (2) *genetic testing of adults* to determine if they are carriers of a particular disease-related gene that may be prevalent in their family or ethnic group. In the first case, prenatal screening originally served only one purpose, to allow parents to abort a fetus if its deformity was thought to be too burdensome for the infant or for the family and society. Obviously, given the general Christian opposition to abortion, prenatal screening with the intention of aborting deformed fetuses would seem to be immoral. However, some believe that the case of a severely deformed fetus falls into a gray area with other, more complex abortion cases (e.g., rape, incest, or threat to the mother's life).

More importantly, given the beginnings of medical or surgical procedures that can be done *in utero* to correct genetic defects, prenatal diagnosis increasingly is becoming a tool for potential therapy, rather than a diagnosis for abortion. Those parents who may have some reason to suspect genetic disease might wish to undergo amniocentesis, chorionic villus sampling, and/or sonogram in order to be prepared. Even if no therapy is possible prenatally, parents might plan to have their high-risk baby born in a more sophisticated neonatal intensive care unit where the latest perinatal techniques and therapies are readily available. Thus, the moral issue in prenatal screening is not the information itself but the use that is made of that genetic information.

In terms of the genetic screening of adults, two kinds of issues arise: (1) what to do if the information bodes ill for the chance of producing healthy offspring and (2) confidentiality related to that medical data. What if one discovers that she or he is the carrier of a deadly or debilitating genetic disease and is statistically very likely to pass it on to one's future children? Or what if two people discover that together they have the genetic likelihood of procreating a child who will inherit such a disease? Should the first person forsake marriage altogether? Or should he, as well as the second couple, forgo having their own biological children? Or, as some few suggest, should they go ahead and conceive and have prenatal testing done, with the intention of aborting if the fetus is deformed? Here the moral question of abortion butts up against the value of having information garnered from prenatal diagnosis.

In no way do we want to say that disabled persons in our midst are any less human, any less personal, any less an image of God, or in any way unworthy of having been born into our community. Still, all things being equal, there does seem to be some moral responsibility to bring into the world children who are as healthy and physically fit as possible, both for their own sakes and for the genetic health of the human family (sometimes called the "gene pool"). Information itself is neither moral nor immoral. What we do with that information is the pertinent moral issue.

Does the information garnered from genetic screening belong exclusively to the person screened, or do other family members have a right to that information, particularly if it is about a family-rooted genetic mutation or defect? Who is obliged to tell the rest of the family? The individual? I would say yes, though situational factors of each family must be considered. The physician or genetic counselor? Arguably no, unless the initial patient grants permission. Similar questions of confidentiality arise with any medical information that has wider public health implications. There is a creative moral tension between the individual's right to confidentiality and the community's right to information that might protect public health or safety. Most churches tilt toward the right of the individual or couple to make their own decisions about genetic information and related procreation.

Government intervention and coercion in very personal matters of health and sexual mating give us pause, particularly given our twentieth-century experiences of Nazism, fascism, and Soviet and Chinese communism. Lest we forget, there were also medical experiments and involuntary sterilizations done on "captive" populations in hospitals and mental institutions in the United States in recent decades as well. To avoid potential social evils, it seems best, for the most part, to err on the side of confidentiality and privacy in terms of one's medical and genetic records.

Q. **36. What about gene splicing and therapies? Is it ever moral to "play God" and tamper with "mother nature"?**

Gene therapy, which is largely in its infancy, is roughly divided into two types, those genetic interventions designed to eliminate either the symptoms or root cause of diseases and abnormalities (i.e., *negative eugenics*) and those genetic manipulations designed to program improvements into the human genome map, to create a sturdier, smarter, "better" hybrid human being (i.e., *positive eugenics*). Most Christian denominations see no major moral roadblock to negative eugenic therapy to ameliorate symptoms or to eliminate specific genetic diseases from the human gene pool. Because not all diseases are caused by a single isolated gene and because altering one element on the DNA chain may have adverse side effects in other aspects of one's genetically programmed life, researchers and future therapists must be careful not to overestimate their abilities. Provided gene therapy research proceeds cautiously and with built-in safety checks and balances, there is no fundamental moral objection to creatively cooperating with God in healing or eradicating disease.

There are more ethical concerns when we step onto the slippery slope of positive eugenics. This kind of genetic manipulation leaves the realm of "therapy," cure of illness or disease, and enters the realm of creation. While expressions such as "playing God" and "fooling with mother nature" may be a bit strong, we are right to be cautious, even suspicious when someone sets out to make a better human being. Whose definition of "better" will be used? Physiologically better or mentally so? Can we build in values, virtues, and character? Who decides what constitutes the improved version of the species? Scientists alone? Government? A popular poll or democratic vote? This is not to say that all efforts to improve our capacities (e.g., to withstand climate changes, to better metabolize food, to resist germs and viruses more effectively) would necessarily be evil or immoral. But as a community we ought to be extremely cautious about schemes to improve the species, whether certain individuals and groups or the human race as a whole. Serving as stewards of God's genetic creation, we are called to be responsibly innovative, mindful of our own limitations.

The whole field of genetic engineering has awesome potential, for good or for ill. It is important that "we the people" ask the ethical questions alongside the scientific discoveries and advances. This dialogue between science and ethics will enhance the potential for thoughtful and creative human cooperation with the divine creator, God willing.

Q. **37. Recently a government committee recommended guidelines for research on human embryos and aborted fetuses. Is such research right or wrong?**

You really have two questions mixed together here. Several years

ago a study panel at the National Institutes of Health recommended that government approval and funding could be given for
research involving the tissue of *already dead* fetuses. In the final
stages of certain drug testing it would be beneficial to test results on
human tissue rather than that of lower animal species. The argument to allow such testing on already deceased fetuses parallels that
for the donation of organs or tissue from a homicide victim or a
person tragically killed in a drunk driving accident. No one is condoning the murder or the reckless driving, but the dead person's
organs or tissue may greatly benefit a transplant recipient or further scientific knowledge. One need not applaud murder or drunk
driving in order to validate use of the human remains that result
from such unfortunate occurrences. In like manner, the federal
panel argued that one need not approve or applaud abortion in
order to justify using the fetal tissue in transplants or research to
benefit others.

A minority dissenting report was issued arguing that there is no
inherent connection between abortions, whether spontaneous or
induced, and the subsequent use of the fetal tissue. However, if this
therapeutic use contributes to society's becoming more complacent
about the number of elective abortions performed—believing that at
least the tissue is of benefit to transplant recipients and researchers—
then in some sense the valid use of fetal tissue bears on the issue of
abortion. Thus, the dissenters concluded that fetal tissue ought not
be used unless it is clear that it comes solely from noninduced abortions, that is, spontaneous miscarriages only.

Moral arguments for the use of embryos for research or potential
transplant purposes would be the same, provided that the embryos
are already dead. However, in 1994 a federal panel suggested that
viable or live embryos, particularly those left frozen after *in vitro* fertilization attempts, might be thawed, kept alive, and used in experimental research for a period of about fourteen days. The panel
argued that prior to the development of the neural tube (origin of
the spinal column and brain stem), one cannot be said to have the
necessary structures to be truly personal. The gene package is
there, but until the point at which the embryo develops the rudi-
ments of a neurological network, it cannot truly be considered an
individual. If brain activity is the measure of life/death at life's
outer edge, one might argue that prior to brain structures and activ-

ity at life's beginning edge, one is not yet "alive." Others suggest that the time of implantation, approximately two weeks after conception, merits consideration as the point at which the embryo becomes a distinct individual entity or "person." Christians might use the term "soul" or "spirit" for this dividing line, though many argue that the time of conception is the best place to posit this infusion of life, personhood, or soul.

In summary, for those who hold that ensoulment or personhood occurs at conception and who therefore are opposed to all abortions, all research using "live" or viable embryos is absolutely immoral, regardless of the time frame. For those who believe that prior to rudimentary brain structures an embryo "experiences" nothing and in some sense is not yet "alive," research is possible provided the results sought cannot be gained by use of lower animals and that the embryos, once used, are disposed of properly and with a modicum of respect. The same conclusion would hold for those who adopt implantation as the personhood threshold. It is important to note that the proposed 1994-95 guidelines were neither accepted nor implemented. It appears that current moral opinion hovers somewhere near the official Catholic belief:

> If the embryos are living, whether viable or not, they must be respected just like any other human person; experimentation on embryos which is not directly therapeutic is illicit. (*Donum Vitae*, 1987, I.4)

Q. 38. Given the high cost of medical care today, including cutting-edge technology, what does Christianity say about healthcare reform? Is our healthcare system O.K., or is some kind of reform really needed?

This is a question focused more on healthcare in the United States. Christians in the other English-speaking industrialized nations where this book might find its way have already dealt, more or less effectively, with the issue of universal access to healthcare. On any given day in the United States, some thirty to thirty-seven million Americans have no healthcare insurance or guaranteed coverage. A further fifteen to thirty million people have inadequate coverage. A disproportionate number of these uninsured citizens are women and children, particularly those of ethnic minorities. If we add those two numbers together, we find that about one-fifth of the entire population of this richest nation on earth does not have access to proper healthcare. Emergency rooms at many of our central city hospitals do accept those who cannot pay, but often such bandaid care comes too late. In terms of prenatal care, basic immunizations, regular checkups, and dental hygiene, people without health insurance or a benefits package often fall between the healthcare cracks.

At the same time, medical costs continue to escalate for the rest of us at the same time that our healthcare benefits frequently are being trimmed. In 1980 the average per-person cost for healthcare coverage in this country was $1,016. By 1990 that had risen 150 percent to $2,425. If we do nothing to check the rising cost of healthcare, to curb abuses, and to reduce the amount of costly paperwork, then by the year 2000 healthcare will cost $5,515 per person, with those forty-five to sixty-seven million uninsured or underinsured persons still left out of the pool. The basic question for us to ask, as good Christians and citizens of this richest industrial nation on earth, seems to be, Is this the best we can do?

Do people have a right to healthcare? I think the Christian and humane response is a resounding yes. Like the Good Samaritan, who went out of his way to care for a stranger who had been beaten (Luke 10:29–37), we are called to carry on the Lord's ministry of healing. One of the corporal works of mercy, from Jesus' own account of the last judgment, is caring for the sick (Matt. 25:36). Whether one looks at religious decrees such as Pope John XXIII's often quoted *Peace on Earth* (1963, #11), or at international secular documents such as the *United Nations Declaration of Human Rights* (1948), one finds this core human mandate:

> Everyone has the right to a standard of living adequate for the health and well-being of himself and of his family, including food, clothing, housing and medical care and necessary social services, and the right to security in the event of unemployment, sickness, disability, widowhood, old age or other lack of livelihood in circumstances beyond his control. (*U.N. Declaration of Human Rights*, 25)

This does not mean that everyone has a right to "free" healthcare. All things being equal, most of us earn our health insurance through the sweat of our brow. Nor does everyone have a right to any and all medical technology. Medical resources are not unlimited. No one has a right to a limitless portion of the finite healthcare pie. But, barring famine or great depression in the land, every person in the community is entitled to have access to a reasonable package of healthcare services, at an affordable price, that remains across one's life span, whether one is working, changing jobs, retired, or unemployed and whether one is young or old, healthy or sickly. How to finance such access is certainly debatable. The individual citizen, employer, society at large (charity and volunteerism), healthcare professionals, insurers, and government all have roles to play in securing and financing affordable healthcare for all.

In the summer of 1993, shortly before the Clinton healthcare proposal was unveiled, and long before it went down to defeat in Congress, the Catholic bishops in this country proposed a set of eight core values that ought to undergird any just and equitable healthcare reform: (1) universal access, (2) priority concern for the poor, (3) respect for life, (4) a comprehensive basic benefits package, (5) pluralism of provider options, (6) equitable financing, (7) cost containment, and (8) quality care for all. It seems to me that these are sound, broadly based moral concerns that should be shared by all, regardless of one's political party or religious affiliation. What a reform plan should look like, how it ought to be managed, and how it can best be financed are all questions open to honest debate.

Q. **39. What do you think about the Oregon Plan, where an attempt was made to "ration" healthcare to those on welfare?**

The term "rationing" is often used to scare us, as if currently there is no rationing of healthcare resources. There already is, and always has been, rationing or apportioning of finite medical resources. Not everyone's insurance covers the same kinds or amount of healthcare. Some have a dental plan, others don't. Some have coverage for pregnancy, psychological counseling, and organ transplants, while others have plans that exclude these. Wealthy people can purchase additional insurance or pay for health services out of pocket; others can't afford the extras. For example, elective cosmetic surgeries—facelifts, tummy tucks, breast implants, liposuction—are rarely covered by insurance.

The fact that most health insurance packages demand larger patient copayments these days is not solely designed to save insurers' money. It is partly designed to help us, the consumers/patients, to realize that healthcare costs a lot and that none of us is entitled to unbridled access to any and all medical technology and procedures. Until recently most ethicists taught that "extraordinary" or disporportionate medical means are optional (see Q. 23). More and more are now suggesting that if a medical therapy is truly disproportionate (too little benefit for too great a burden), perhaps it is unjust and wasteful to opt for it at all. Talk of healthcare rationing merely acknowledges that healthcare personnel, equipment, and dollars are not unlimited.

So, in theory, the Oregon Plan makes a lot of sense. I would rather have us discuss our healthcare limits more openly and make some community-wide decisions about what basic benefits ought to be guaranteed to all versus what items ought to remain optional. But in practice the Oregon Plan seems to put the cart before the horse. The ordinary Oregonian, who had his or her own health insurance, was not included in the initial rationing venture. So too, lobbyists for senior citizens and persons with disabilities managed to get these groups exempted from the rationing pool. The only persons left whose access to healthcare would be constrained by rationing were the poor, who had no lobby working in their behalf, largely single women and their dependent children. Various religious groups took opposite sides on this question. I think most of their division hovered around this *in theory* versus *in practice* debate. If citizens of an entire state or region were willing to decide together what benefits would or would not be available to all—those with private insurance as well as those subsidized by the government—then a degree of equity and justice would be introduced into the rationing process. With such safeguards in place, rationed and/or managed healthcare might be a reasonable, fair, and morally justified option.

It seems to me that the most immoral option in the whole healthcare debate is to do nothing. Greed, selfishness, hardball lobbying by insurance companies, and partisan politics blocked any kind of reform in 1994. Without baptizing any approach as "the Christian model," I think we have a Christian and a civic obligation to engage in the healthcare debate. The common good of all is tied up in how well we foster the dignity and rights of those who are voiceless and powerless in the debate.

Q. **40. Do you have any final thoughts you want to share about healthcare ethics in the 1990s?**

Thanks for the opportunity to express briefly three overarching concerns that I have regarding morality and healthcare. First, *death* is not the ultimate enemy. Dying is natural and inevitable. It comes to us all. Dying is the necessary last phase of this life, ushering us into eternity, the fullness of life. For Christians this ought to be obvious. The death and resurrection of Jesus are the path and pattern we each must follow. Time and again I am amazed by the number of Christians who border on being vitalists, that is, fighting to keep themselves or their loved ones "alive," hooked up to machines, at all costs. The prudential weighing of benefit and burden is truly the Christian way to show reasonable respect for this phase of life, without denying that we are all bound for glory, on an eternal life journey through and beyond dying.

Second, *health* is an elusive reality. In 1946 the World Health Organization offered an overly optimistic definition: *Health* is "the state of complete physical, mental, and social well-being, and not merely the absence of disease or infirmity." While such a definition is helpful in reminding us that our healing efforts ought to be person-centered, not merely disease-focused, ultimately such a definition is too lofty. "The state of complete physical, mental, and social well-being" is a definition of paradise or heaven on earth. Securing that is far beyond the ability of any physician, healthcare facility, or insurance program to guarantee. What we ought to be able to guarantee is not perfect health but access to a share in those earthly benefits that will foster reasonably good health—food, clothing, shelter, basic medical care, education, human freedoms, and the adequate means to obtain and maintain these.

Finally, while medical science and technology have discovered awesome things about human biology and health, healthcare is as much a human art as it is a technical science, if not more. When physicians suggest that one "has a 60-40 chance of recovery," or "will likely be able to walk again," these are human judgment calls, "guesstimates" at best. My point here is twofold: (1) Put your trust in God, come what may—not solely in doctors or in surgery, medicines, and medical science. (2) Know that human *caring*, what we've often called "bedside manner," is as much a part of the healing arts as are our attempts at *curing* one's disease, if not more. Healthcare ethics is about the medical art of curing where possible, and the human art of caring always.

Issues in Sexual Morality

Q. 41. When I was growing up it seemed as if the most serious kind of sin was anything to do with sex. Now it seems as if "anything goes." What do you have to say about sexual morality in the 1990s?

Everywhere you look—newspapers, popular magazines, advertisements, billboards, films, television, and media talk shows—our contemporary culture seems to be heavily, even overly, focused on sex. At one time I used to preach that "we Americans are obsessed with sex. We use it to sell cars, clothing, fragrances, and almost any other product." At that phase in my life I was trying to say that sex is out of proportion in our society, as if it's just not that central or important. I was wrong! No, I'm not saying that sex is number one, or the most important thing in life. But *sexuality*, with the emphasis on the "uality" part, is rather important, right up there at number two, three, or four. Thomas Aquinas affirmed that next to the desire to stay alive, the drives to procreate and to live in communion with others are deeply rooted in the human psyche, by nature and by God (*Summa Theologica* I, II q. 94).

Notice I didn't say "sex" but "sexuality." That's a broader concept. In a recent study the Catholic bishops of the United States define these terms as follows, paralleling the opinions of mainline Protestant churches:

Sexuality refers to a fundamental component of personality in and through which we, as male or female, experience our relatedness to self, others, the world, and even God. *Sex* refers *either* to the biological aspects of being male or female (i.e., a synonym for one's gender) *or* to the expressions of sexuality, which have physical, emotional, and spiritual dimensions, particularly genital actions resulting in sexual intercourse and/or orgasm. (*Human Sexuality*, 1991, p. 9)

If you were to ask me, "Is sex that important?" I might say, "No, not really." But if you were to ask me whether *sexuality* is so important as to be the center of attention in so much of our media, I guess I'd have to say, "Yes, sexuality is really core in each of us, for our self-identity and for our human relationships."

That said, I do think that our culture is too focused on *sex*, the "doing it" dimension, and not concerned enough about *sexuality*—who we are underneath and how we affect others—those fuller dimensions of being embodied, sensual, sexual human beings. I think that in our hunger to love and to be loved, to touch and to be touched, to affirm and to be affirmed, all of which are natural desires and good, we may too easily settle for the "quick fix," as if genuine love can be reduced to a moment of orgasm. At times the Christian tradition itself has tended to focus too much on sex and primarily on sexual sins rather than sexual virtues. Still, I think our underlying concern has always been to enhance the dignity of the individuals involved, to preserve the sacredness of marriage, and to foster the responsible use of our procreative potential.

Q. **42. Are you saying, then, that sex is morally permissible only in a committed married relationship?**

Yes, according to the scriptures and traditional teaching in the mainline Christian churches, sexual intercourse is a blessing and a privilege reserved to married couples. Why? Because we Christians believe that God, who is Love and the author of Life, has inscribed in the act of sex two core meanings, love and life. Sexual intercourse is at one and the same time an expression of deep interpersonal intimacy and commitment—what is often called the *unitive* or *two-in-one-flesh* meaning—as well as an act that is potentially life-giving—the *procreative* meaning.

When two persons marry, they pledge to be there for each other, in good times and in bad, in sickness and in health, for richer or poorer, until death. It is within that lifelong covenant relationship that sex makes sense as an expression of their intimate and faithful love and as the context in which babies are best conceived. So, complete sexual union (i.e., sexual intercourse) belongs within marriage. Outside of that context, something is missing, either the depth and duration of commitment or the responsible setting in which procreation becomes appropriate.

Q. **43. You say "complete sexual union belongs within marriage." What do you mean? How far can you go *before* marriage or if you're not intending to be married?**

That's probably the most frequently asked question in teenage youth ministry, in single adult seminars, and in support groups for divorced people—How far can we go? I'd like to respond in two ways. First, let's go back to the broader concept of sexuality, which we defined above. Because I am male, influenced by that XY chromosome, in *every* cell of my body, almost every human relationship I have has a sexual dimension. If an attractive woman or a pleasant looking man shakes my hand, smiles at me, gives me a hug, or speaks kindly to me, I respond. I don't mean that I respond genitally necessarily, but I do have some kind of interior "feeling" that either draws me toward that person or repels me. Part of that subtle attraction or repulsion is *sexual*, that seemingly magical, though largely hormonal, dimension in each of us. It is, in part, sexual attraction that prompts an awkward adolescent boy to risk the taunting of his male peers in order to lumber across the gymnasium to ask a gangly pubescent girl to dance. It is, in part, sexual attraction that prompts a middle-aged married couple to "dress up" for their anniversary, to go out for a romantic dinner, and to dance the night away to "golden oldie" tunes. And it is, in part, sexual attraction that prompts a lonely widowed woman or man to attend a coed card party, bus trip, or special event sponsored by the senior center.

We are inherently and abidingly sexual beings from the womb to the tomb. Once, when an older priest was asked by a young seminarian, "When do these sexual urges go away?" he responded, "I think about three hours after you're in the grave." That is true for all of us—married or single, old or young, divorced, widowed, or avowedly celibate. Sexuality and its accompanying feelings, fantasies, and urges are one sign that we are alive, healthy, and embodied, the way God intended us to be. These are not inherently "bad

feelings" or "dirty thoughts," as some of us were taught in the con-
fessional practices of a bygone era. Sexual feelings are one dimension, one of the core "attracting" stimuli in the divine call to be
lovers, to be caregivers, to be involved in the lives of our families,
friends, coworkers, fellow believers, and the whole human family of
God.

But being sexual in this general sense doesn't really resolve the
action question—How far can we go?—in terms of sexual touches,
genital touches, physical expressions of and responses to those
broader sexual feelings. It has been the constant tradition of the
Christian churches that the full sexual expression of genital intercourse belongs only in marriage. But that does not mean that
people are to remain untouchable, pristine in a Victorian sense,
until their wedding night. Just as one becomes more vulnerable,
more "naked" in terms of verbal intimacy as one grows deeper into
a human love relationship, so too the physical and symbolic expressions of that relational intimacy become more personal, more sexual in a similarly incremental way.

At this point teenagers often want me to give them a step-by-step
chart. For example, first date = hold hands and kiss on the cheek;
second date = kiss on the lips; third date = cuddle for ten minutes,
clothes on; and so on. There isn't now and never has been the perfect list, despite what some of those old handbooks for boys and
girls might once have decreed. Which sexual, not necessarily genital, expressions of affection are appropriate prior to or outside of
marriage is not resolved by a list of time frames and body parts.

Each couple must discern their own level of intimacy and depth
of commitment and respond accordingly, appropriately. The closer
one is to marriage, the more tender and vulnerable one may be,
such that the wedding night is the next natural step, an ecstatic and
graced experience. The farther one is from marriage, the more we
may be toying with each other's affections, miscommunicating our
own level of commitment, and implying things we don't really mean
if we are too physically or sexually intimate. So while the Christian
tradition calls and challenges us to abstain from sexual intercourse
before we are married, that does not mean we are to be touchless,
kissless, and puritanical in our single relationships. The virtue for
this art of prudent discernment is called "chastity."

Q. **44. What do you mean by "chastity"? I always thought chastity, celibacy, and virginity were the same thing.**

As the Catholic bishops note in their document entitled *Human Sexuality*:

> Chastity is often misunderstood as simply a suppression or deliberate inhibition of sexual thoughts, feelings, and actions. However, chastity truly consists in the long-term integration of one's thoughts, feelings, and actions in a way that values, esteems, and respects the dignity of oneself and others. (1991, p. 19)

Chastity is less about which actions one does or doesn't do than about self-control, modesty, and being sexually appropriate for who one is in a given relationship. Thus, for a married couple, chastity can mean lots of healthy, enjoyable lovemaking, but exclusively with each other. For single people, the question is one of appropriateness—how physical should we be given our level of maturity, intimacy, vulnerability, honesty, and commitment? The old adage "moderation in all things" is applicable here. The truly chaste person is not the uptight or prudish person but the one who can respond honestly and appropriately in each relationship. Chastity is also the virtue involved when we draw appropriate sexual and touch boundaries at work or school, with friends, and in other nonromantic and nonspousal relationships.

Q. **45. Let me see if I understand you. You are saying that people ought to abstain from sex before marriage, aren't you? That's still the sin of fornication, isn't it?**

You asked two questions for the price of one. My response to your first question is yes, the Christian tradition still defends abstinence from sexual intercourse before marriage as the best and only moral course for dating couples. However, I think that we can and ought to be more positive in our presentation of abstinence. For too many people it simply means "doing without." Abstinence is not just saying no to genital sexual activity, but in some profound sense saying yes to one's own sexual future and future spouse. Saving oneself sexually for marriage is a way of saying, "No for now, but a fuller yes for later; no to the pleasure of the moment, but yes to the future expression of my love for a lifetime."

As much as I encourage young people, indeed all single people to wait, and even as I invite all parents, teachers, and mentors to encourage such chaste abstinence, we must be careful *not* to imply that the loss of one's virginity, the decision to overstep these moral boundaries, is some kind of unforgivable sin. A number of sexuality education programs describe one's recommitment to chastity after having been prematurely sexually active as a kind of "second virginity." While our bodily organs cannot regain their virginal state, our souls or spirits can always be mended, healed, and made whole again. Where sin or human mistakes abound, God's mercy and forgiveness abound more. Second chances—and third and fourth and fifth—are always possible. The corollary to the call to mature sexual chastity is the promise of God's unconditional love and forgiveness, the opportunity to start again, if one has chosen inappropriately and sinned.

That brings me to your second question, about "the sin of fornication." There's no doubt, in the scriptures and Christian tradition, that all sex outside of marriage has been dubbed "fornication," with the subcategory "adultery" being used if either partner or both partners are married. While that language is not altogether incorrect, I find the term "fornication" offensive to many and, in some instances, too simplistic or loaded a term for the complexity of the situation and the subjective sincerity of many of the couples involved. No, that doesn't mean I'm defending sex outside of marriage. It's just that there seem to be degrees of moral difference between a couple making love within days prior to their wedding vows and a prostitute or gigolo selling sexual services to a customer and two teenagers groping their way through a puppy-love sexual encounter in the backseat of a car. All are instances of sex outside of marriage. According to the Christian tradition each act is objectively wrong, though each has its own distinct situational features.

I'm not convinced that the somewhat cold term "fornication" describes accurately or with sufficient nuance the almost married couple or the naïvely premature teen encounter. So too, while the term "fornication" may better describe the sex-for-sale example, I think the exchange of money, treating sex as a commodity, and the socioeconomic factors often linked to the life of streetcorner prostitutes, female and male, make this a more tragic case, one requiring more pastoral care and challenge than mere moral labeling. In short, while "fornication" has been our traditional term for all sex outside of marriage, I would be more interested in dealing with the messiness—including the degree of sinfulness—in each instance, without seeking some neat and largely pejorative label to drop on all instances of premarital or nonmarital sex.

As we discussed earlier (QQ. 11, 13–14), declaring an action objectively immoral is not identical to calling it "sinful" or the person involved "a sinner." Remember that sin—one's moral/spiritual standing before God—also involves the depth and degree of moral responsibility of those involved. This we cannot judge in the abstract. So I would prefer to say that, according to our Christian tradition, sex outside of marriage is seen as always objectively immoral, leaving the determination of sinfulness to each person's own prayerful discernment with God, often guided by one's spiritual director, pastor, confessor, a trusted friend, or mentor.

Q. **46. You briefly mentioned "adultery." I know the church believes that is wrong. So do I. But what else can be said about the morality of sex within marriage? As long as you're married, does anything go?**

I have often heard well-intentioned marriage counselors or pastoral ministers say this. I confess to being ill-at-ease with a response such as, "as long as you're married anything goes." While there is an element of truth there, it has too often been misconstrued by abusive husbands to demand their marital rights by force—often verbal coercion, sometimes actual physical violence. Forcing sex upon one's spouse, particularly through physical or verbal abuse, can be a species of "rape," surely *not* an example of spousal rights or marital lovemaking. (See also Q. 94.)

Ideally, within a healthy marriage, one finds two people who seek to enjoy sexual intimacy together, to mutually satisfy one another, and to discover ways to grow closer in verbal as well as physical intimacy. Someone once said that the largest sex organ in the body is the head. It is in the human brain that we think sexual thoughts, feel sexual feelings, and ultimately initiate, command, and respond to sexual activity. Therefore, it is as much in the meeting of the minds as in the coming together of other body parts that true mating and lovemaking happen. Sensitivity to each other's wishes, desires, suggestions, as well as to each other's inhibitions, misgivings, and personal tastes or moral boundaries must be paramount.

Some married couples seem to be able to do a variety of intimate sexual actions, under the umbrella of foreplay or extended lovemaking, but are reluctant to discuss their sexual desires, pleasures, and actions. Being able to talk about what they do, or would like to do, is an essential step in developing a trusting, caring, truly intimate relationship, in which sexual expressions find their natural and rightful place.

Documents from various Christian churches are not terribly explicit in describing what may or may not be done in terms of sexplay within the context of marital lovemaking. I think this is as it should be. In the Gospels Jesus says very little about marriage beyond the call to mutual fidelity (Mark 10:1–12; Matt. 5:31; 19:1–9; Luke 16:18) and nothing at all about sexual activity. I think the church should be similarly circumspect when it comes to describing, condoning, or condemning specific arousal techniques and the like. The focus of Christian teaching is more about loving attitudes and virtues—fidelity, commitment, sensitivity, communication, mutuality, generosity, self-sacrifice, trust, humility—than about specific marital sexual practices. Whatever the couple mutually discern as enhancing their experience of two-in-one-flesh intimacy would seem to be moral, provided it is within the context of marital sexual intercourse and an ongoing effort to keep the channels of interpersonal communication open between them.

Q. **47. Then what about contraception? If a married couple both want to space their children, is it moral to use the pill, a condom, or other aids to prevent conception?**

You've cornered me there. If mutuality and communal discernment are the moral decision making process, then you're rightly asking if a couple may decide that "for them" contraception is the loving, caring, morally acceptable thing to do. Here the most honest answer I can give, given the title of this book, is either no or yes.

From an official Roman Catholic perspective the answer is clearly and unequivocally no. It is not morally justifiable to use the pill, a condom, or any other form of direct contraception. Since the early 1930s, when Pope Pius XI offered some lengthy reflections on the meaning and boundaries of Christian marriage, the Catholic church has consistently taught that marital sexual intercourse has two inseparable meanings, which we noted earlier, (1) the unitive or two-in-one-flesh love meaning and (2) the procreative potential or life-giving meaning. It is official Catholic teaching that each time a married couple make love they ought to be open to both meanings. By "open" is meant that the couple will do nothing *directly* to inhibit or go against either meaning, committed love or potential procreation.

However, in 1951 Pope Pius XII openly acknowledged that for a variety of good reasons, a married couple rightly might want to make love, while forgoing the possibility, for the present, of conceiving a child. The use of what was then called "the rhythm method" was deemed a morally valid means for married couples to adopt in spacing children, provided their reasons were conducive to the good of the whole marriage and not merely self-seeking or materialistic. In the decades since then the Catholic church has reiterated this view in such documents as *Humanae Vitae* (1968) and *Familiaris Consortio* (1981).

In recent years medical science has improved the methods for discovering when a woman has ovulated (i.e., originally called the rhythm method). Thus, the method now known as "natural family planning" is based more on verifiable physical and hormonal data than on an assumed twenty-eight day cycle and calendar charting. It is the official stance of the Catholic church that natural family planning allows a couple to make love on infertile days in the wife's cycle, which is in no way a *direct* assault on or suppression of her fertility nor an impeding of the marital act's natural processes. In a sense, it is as if God built in a natural or biological loophole, a window of opportunity, which allows married couples to make love while being open to procreation, with the possibility of the latter being very unlikely.

The reason I said that the response to your contraception question is either no or yes is that this book purports to be about issues in "Christian," not exclusively "Roman Catholic," morality. I am a Catholic priest and moral theologian. Thus, I am rightly obliged to show *obsequium*—variously described as respect, deference, or even religious submission—to my church's official teaching, on this matter as on other moral issues. And so, with due respect for my own tradition, I tactfully wish to add the following information for those other Christians who have selected this book to aid them in moral decision making, and for those members of my own tradition who seek broader information in their ongoing formation of conscience.

A number of prominent Christian ethicists (e.g., the late Paul Ramsey, James Gustafson, James B. Nelson) as well as Christians of other mainline denominations accept to a large degree the basic twofold meaning of sexual intercourse proposed by the Roman Catholic tradition, namely, the lovemaking and the life-giving dimensions. However, as far back as the Anglican Conference at Lambeth (1929) some Christian denominations and their theologians have drawn a different conclusion about the use of contraceptive devices and pharmaceuticals. Ramsey suggested that the two meanings are present across the life span of a married couple's sexual activity, but that at any given period within the marriage or in any given act of sexual intercourse one or the other meaning may be dominant. He called these the "spheres" of one's marriage.

Thus, during the early childbearing years of a marriage a couple may be making love with the specific intention of procreating a child. So too, those potentially infertile couples who seek medical assistance to conceive, for that period of time, may be focusing directly, almost exclusively on trying to co-create a baby. This would not mean that they are any less a loving couple, but that their lovemaking activity is timed, spaced, and focused primarily around ovulation, sperm count, and trying to conceive.

By contrast, during pregnancy, when celebrating an anniversary, after menopause, or during most of a couple's married life, the focus of their conjugal activity may be more on the unitive or two-in-one-flesh dimension of sexually being together. In the same way, when a couple's marriage is "on the rocks" or if they are undergoing counseling in an effort to save their marriage, sexual intimacy, when the mood is right, may be a particularly helpful means of communication. However, becoming pregnant at such times could be ill-advised, more of an added stressful burden than a blessing, for an already shaky marriage. At such times of mutual joy or struggle the experience of sexual intercourse, of one person being inside the other, of mutual self-giving, may incarnate their love and fidelity. This allows the couple to celebrate and enhance the intimacy they already share or are striving to rekindle. In a very real sense they are "making" love or trying to deepen their love in this symbolic covenant-renewing act. Procreation either may be impossible at this time or psychologically and relationally inappropriate.

In either instance or sphere of marriage—one in which procreation is the primary focus or one in which lovemaking is a given couple's main intent—Ramsey and others believe that such sexual intimacy is moral. Thus, there are a significant number of Protestant and Orthodox denominations as well as a sizable percentage of Catholics who believe that the answer to your question would be yes. Direct contraception can be a moral option, provided one's reasons are focused on the holistic good of the spouses and their marriage. All would morally differentiate between those methods of contraception which may abort (I.U.D.'s, RU-486, or the D.E.S. pill) and those which merely prevent conception from occurring (condoms, diaphragms, and other barrier methods; and estrogen-oriented contraceptive pills). Within the space constraints of this small book, this is as honest, complete, and tactful a response as I can give to your question about contraception.

Q. 48. Thanks for your candor. What about artificial insemination, test-tube babies, and surrogate mothers? Are any, some, or all of these reproductive technologies moral to use?

On 27 July 1978, the first so-called test-tube baby, Louise Brown, was born in Oldham, England. In a laboratory petrie dish, an ovum from her mother had been combined with sperm from her father, incubated for a few hours, and then implanted into her mother, where it (i.e., Baby Louise) matured until birth. This whole process is known as *in vitro* fertilization or I.V.F. It is one of the amazing possibilities of modern medical technology designed to assist couples who have trouble conceiving or carrying their own offspring to term.

As far back as the 1930s medical science had developed the abil-

ity to artificially inseminate a woman by injecting her with a sufficient quantity of her husband's sperm (AIH) or, in some cases, with
the semen of an anonymous donor (AID—*not* to be confused with
the deadly disease called AIDS). If you do any reading in this area
or if you yourself enter into the realm of fertility clinics and specialists, you will soon learn that the two main classes of treatment
options are (1) *homologous* procedures—those which use *only* the
couple's own biological materials (sperm, ova, and uterus)—and
(2) *heterologous* procedures—those which introduce a third person's
biological parts into the process (donor sperm, donor ova, and/or a
surrogate womb).

Any discussion of the moral rightness or wrongness of such technology has to start with the very real, often painful situation of the
married couple who have difficulty conceiving the "natural" or
"old-fashioned" way. In a culture such as ours, which is so focused
on success, on getting ahead, and in which most people hope to
pass on the fruit of their success to their children, the inability to
conceive or to carry a child to term is often a painful and embarrassing experience. The inability to conceive can wreak havoc on a
woman's or a man's self-esteem, their sense of being feminine or
masculine, even on their marital communication and fidelity. Pres-
sures from others—parents seeking grandchildren, friends asking
When? or Why not? and even the annual I.R.S. question about the
number of dependents to declare—make an already awkward and
hurtful situation even more difficult.

Couples who seek help from fertility clinics and specialists are
good people, people who desire the blessing and privilege of par-
enthood very much. Empathy, compassion, and gentleness are
called for from all outsiders. It might be well for each of us to ask
ourselves if we, however unintentionally, have increased the burden
or suffering of some relative or friend who remains childless. Bearing one's own biological children is a great gift, but not always biologically possible, not an automatic expectation, as so many
married couples have discovered.

Within this context of empathy and compassion we can now look
at the moral issues of the technologies themselves. It is the position
of the Catholic church that all conception and procreation ought to
occur as the result of two-in-one-flesh marital sexual intercourse.
Remember the unitive/procreative material in the previous ques-

tion. The official Catholic position is that each and every act of sexual intercourse must contain both meanings, lovemaking and potential giving of life. Gathering sperm—most often done through solitary sex (i.e., masturbation)—and then injecting it into the woman with a syringe seems to interrupt or intrude upon the intimacy between the couple which lovemaking symbolizes. So too with *in vitro* fertilization. When one surgically retrieves eggs from the woman, mixes them with semen in the lab, and then injects them into the woman, the laboratory seems to have superseded the couple in this act of conception. Add to this a third party, whether donor of ova, donor of sperm, or surrogate mother (in whose uterus this artificially conceived embryo will grow to term), and one can say, in some sense, that the couple is no longer procreating their own offspring. Medical science is doing it for them, with or without their biological contribution, certainly not requiring their two-in-one-flesh lovemaking at all.

For this reason the official Catholic position says that fertilization is morally right only when it is the result of marital sexual intercourse. To conceive an embryo by any other means—whether the material and procedures are homologous or heterologous—is morally wrong. In addition to the two intrinsic meanings of the sex act, the Catholic church also focuses on the inherent and abiding dignity of the person who will be conceived and the stability of the marriage and nuclear family in which she or he is to be nurtured. In a 1987 Vatican document on the topic, one reads that ideally every child has a right to be conceived and brought into the world in marriage and from marriage, with the emphasis being on the conjugal act of the married couple, not its laboratory extension.

But are the people involved in such technology sincere, whether the couple, donors, surrogates, or physicians and lab technicians? Of course they are. Do they mean any harm by seeking the aid of medical technology to assist in conceiving their own children? Of course not. Their sincerity and dedication are most often admirable. But, as we noted in questions 13–14, a good intention or sincerely "meaning well" is not the sole measure of whether an act is objectively right or wrong. Sincerity impacts whether a person is morally culpable, what we called the *subjective* dimension, but not whether the act in question is *objectively* right.

Q. **49. But just as there was another moral opinion on the subject of contraception, is there a mainline Protestant view on reproductive technology as well?**

It's important to note that "Protestant" is not the name of one church or a single denomination. It is an umbrella term for all those various Christian churches that emerged out of the Reformation or protest movement of the 1500s. Not all Protestant churches hold the same moral viewpoint. In some areas of theology or ethics a given Protestant church might hold a view closer to the Catholic tradition than to some other members of the broader Protestant communion. Still, on this question of reproductive technologies, many Christian churches believe that the Catholic view is too restrictive. When it comes to the use of *homologous* techniques, that is, those in which the ovum, sperm, and uterus are those of the married couple themselves, there seems to be relatively little moral objection. However, when a married couple start to involve the biological material of third parties, what we called *heterologous* procedures, then many Protestant scholars join their Catholic counterparts in raising ethical concerns.

How might a husband or wife feel, knowing that the child he or she is helping to raise is genetically part of one's spouse, but not at all of one's own flesh and blood? It would be ideal to say that this would leave no psychic scar, that one's male or female ego could cope well with this. After all, stepparents and adoptive parents do it all the time. But in those situations the child is already here, alive and well. Couples adopt children or take them under their wing because children need a mom and dad. Is there a difference for a couple who says, "We will create such a child, one who is only half of our marriage and half from an anonymous sperm or ovum donor"?

So too, in the short time since surrogate motherhood has been legal, lawsuits have resulted when a woman who donated ova and volunteered or rented her womb later wanted to keep the baby and negate the surrogacy agreement. What are the surrogate's maternal rights, particularly if the child is 50 percent genetically hers? How much of maternal bonding is psychological and how much is biological, hormonal, and inherent in the very process of bearing a child? These are the kinds of questions that cause many ethicists to challenge the wisdom of *heterologous* reproductive technologies.

Although some believe that these questions are not insurmountable, others are convinced that the issues are serious enough to morally prohibit all *heterologous* artificial inseminations and *in vitro* fertilizations.

Finally, whether one is talking *homologous* or *heterologous* procedures, in the process of retrieving ova from the woman for *in vitro* fertilization, it is common practice to remove and fertilize multiple ova, both to increase the chances of implantation and to forestall the need for multiple expensive invasive surgeries. Thus, in almost every attempt to insert embryos, multiple fertilized ova (usually four or more) are injected in the hope that at least one might implant on the uterine wall and begin to grow. Sometimes multiple implantations occur and the woman bears fraternal twins or triplets. But more often only one or even none implants, and the remaining embryos are discharged or "miscarried" naturally. Depending on one's moral view about abortion and about the moral status of pre-born human life, this issue of extra embryos has greater or lesser moral significance. If one believes that an embryo is a "person," ensouled and endowed with rights from the time of conception, then *in vitro* fertilization is a problem. As it is presently practiced, I.V.F. includes the presence of extra embryos, most destined for natural miscarriage if injected, or for long-term limbo status if left frozen in the laboratory for potential later use.

Add to this the question of "ownership" should there be a divorce or if one parent dies, as well as the question of what do do with the embryos should the couple not wish any further *in vitro* attempts, and the issue of "extra embryos" becomes a significant moral question. The case of an American couple who died in a plane crash, leaving two frozen embryos behind in Australia, brought this potential problem to greater public attention. Could their surviving relatives inherit the couple's property? Or were they obliged to find a surrogate to carry one or both embryos to term, in order that these "only-just-begun" offspring could inherit their now-deceased parents' estate? It is sufficient here to note that this is a layered and complicated issue. Adoption (of native or foreign-born children), foster-parenting, and volunteering one's time in such worthy programs as scouting, youth work, and Big Brother or Big Sister programs may be viable alternatives to some of these more questionable reproductive technologies. In all discussions about the use of modern reproductive technologies, we must balance empathy and compassion for the couple involved with thoughtful, objective moral discernment.

Q. 50. I am wondering about homosexuality, which seems to be so prevalent today in our society. Doesn't the Christian tradition say that homosexuality is wrong?

The short answer to your question is that the Christian tradition has generally upheld that homosexual genital actions are wrong but that *being* homosexual, having a gay or lesbian sexual orientation, is *not* morally wrong. Too often people collapse the two into one, assuming either that being homosexual (i.e., having a homosexual orientation) is in itself immoral or else assuming that anyone who is homosexual must also be acting it out genitally (i.e., having/doing homosexual sex). Not so!

Homosexuality can be defined as "a predominant sexual attraction to persons of the same gender, with a proportionate lack of sexual interest in persons of the opposite gender." It's important to realize that not every dimension of "who we are" is within our control. For example, our race, gender, genetic make-up, and basic personality type, to a large extent, are predetermined—by God, the fates, or human nature—before we are born or certainly before we are mature enough to choose for ourselves. The more medical science delves into the origins of homosexuality, the more we are coming to realize that for most gay men and lesbian women their sexual "orientation" is not a matter of choice. Thus, speaking about sexual "preference" seems to be inaccurate. Somewhere along the continuum from childhood through puberty to adulthood a homosexual person *discovers* that he or she is more sexually drawn to people of the same gender. These individuals don't choose this, but *discover* or come to an awareness that their sexual feelings and fantasies are predominantly about people of their own sex or gender.

In the famous Kinsey studies of human sexuality done in the late 1940s and early 1950s, it was proposed that all of us fall somewhere on a sexual orientation spectrum between 0 and 6, with 0 representing those who are exclusively heterosexual and 6 representing those who are exclusively homosexual. Most of us are somewhere in between, leaning toward one or the other dominant orientation. It also appears that some people are truly bi-sexual in orientation; that is, they feel equally sexually attracted to men and women. For this reason, a number of Christian churches have adopted the somewhat helpful distinction between *orientation* or "being homosexual" and *acts* or "doing homosexual genital sex." In speaking of "being" homosexual, the Catholic bishops clearly state in their 1990 document *Human Sexuality*, "Such an orientation in itself, because not freely chosen, is not sinful." Most Christian churches agree that one cannot be held morally accountable for a "discovery," for a dimension of oneself concerning which one has no choice. It is fundamentally important for all Christians to respect the abiding human dignity of all people, regardless of their sexual orientation. This is a matter both of justice and humane and Christian compassion.

Although most Christian churches, including Roman Catholicism, take this fairly benign approach to sexual orientation, they believe that *doing* homosexual sex, as distinct from *being* homosexual, is morally wrong. Biblical witness, reinforced by a fairly constant teaching throughout the Christian tradition, professes that from the beginning God intended humanity to be male and female (Gen. 1:26–27) and that a certain mutuality or complementarity is inherent in sexually differentiated human nature itself. There is a certain heterosexual norm built into us by divine plan. For example, the Lutheran Confessions affirm that human beings "were created to be fruitful and that one sex should have a proper desire for the other. . . . This love of one sex for the other is truly a divine ordinance" (*Apology of the Augsburg Confessions* XXIII, quoted in ELCA, *Human Sexuality*, 1994 Working Draft). Homosexuality is therefore not the norm, not the way nature intended us to be.

It follows then, if sexual intercourse is about two-in-one-flesh intimacy and about an openness to the procreative possibility—as presented earlier—that homosexual genital sex acts are missing at least one of these two requisite dimensions. Gay or lesbian sex has no possibility of being biologically procreative. Some will also suggest that the intimacy between two people of the same sex cannot approach the same depth or duration as that of heterosexual spouses. However, the personal witness of many homosexual couples, particularly in this era of AIDS-related deaths, would seem to contradict or at least challenge this latter presumption.

Q. **51. But didn't you just waltz around the Christian view of homosexuality with your phrases "not the norm" and "not the way nature intended us to be"? Aren't you really saying that being homosexual is "abnormal" and "unnatural"?**

I chose to phrase it more gently because in addition to the question about the morality of homosexual sex acts there is also the very real moral question of how the rest of society treats homosexual persons in our midst. Just as the church has consistently declared that homosexual genital acts are immoral, so do we strongly confront bigotry against gay and lesbian people, homophobia, and so-called gay bashing. "It is deplorable that homosexual persons have been and are the object of violent malice in speech or in action. Such treatment deserves condemnation from the Church's pastors wherever it occurs." So said the Vatican in a 1986 document on pastoral care of homosexual persons. And the American Catholic bishops added:

> We call on all Christians and citizens of good will to confront their own fears about homosexuality and to curb the humor and discrimination that offends homosexual persons. We understand that having a homosexual orientation brings with it enough anxiety, pain, and issues related to self-acceptance without society adding additional prejudicial treatment.

So, I chose my words carefully, preferring "not the norm" and "not the way nature intended us to be" in an effort to engage you and others in conversation, not to prematurely close doors or offend people, whether heterosexual or homosexual.

Q. **52. If I were a homosexual person, that wouldn't give me much comfort. If a person is created homosexual by God or by nature, why is it considered so wrong to act that out sexually?**

Do you remember back in question 9, when we made the distinction between *being* and *doing*? Ideally, who we are or "be" is lived out in the way we act or "do" the events of our lives. If the two are consistent, then we not only *do* right actions, but also *are* morally good people—our objective acts and our subjective self are in sync. You rightly are bringing that concept to bear on the issue of homosexuality.

There are a number of Christian theologians and people in the pews who find the distinction between *being* homosexual in orientation (which is not morally wrong) and *doing* homosexual genital deeds (which is considered always objectively wrong) a bit confusing. It is meant to uphold the centuries-old belief in a heterosexual norm and in marriage as the proper venue for intimate sexual behavior. While not intended to be unkind or overly pejorative about people who discover that they are homosexual in orientation, the distinction is designed to condemn the actions without condemning the person.

But in the years since this orientation versus act distinction was coined (1960s–1990s), a number of theologians, pastoral ministers who work with gay and lesbian people, and homosexual persons themselves have wondered if the distinction can bear the moral weight heaped upon it. If a good, morally upright, prayerful person discovers that he or she is homosexual, isn't that his or her "natural" state? Isn't that person's homosexual orientation "normal" for him or her? And if that is the case, even if heterosexuality is the statistical norm, shouldn't a person be able to act according to who one is? Most who hold such a view quickly add the proviso that homosexual genital actions would be moral only within the context of a committed, monogamous, covenant relationship, akin to a childless marriage. This is sometimes called the "qualified acceptance" position, because it tolerates or accepts homosexual sex by way of exception to the accepted or presumed heterosexual norm.

Other Christians (e.g., United Church of Christ ethicist James B. Nelson) suggest that granting second-class or "also-ran" status to people with a homosexual orientation is demeaning and an inadequate response. Since we do not know what causes someone to be gay or lesbian—genetics, hormones, psychosocial upbringing, or some combination of these factors—why should we automatically put a negative spin on the orientation? Why assume that it is *not* ordained by God or nature? These theologians argue that the true measure of sexual morality ought to be the quality of the relationship, the depth of commitment, and the sexual responsibility of the couple involved. Therefore, if a homosexual orientation is seen as God-given or "natural" for a significant minority of the population, then it ought not merely to be tolerated by way of exception, but rather should be accepted and protected in our society as a valid variation of life-style and sexual response. As the 1994 Evangelical Lutheran "working draft" phrases it:

> Those who have followed this line of reasoning [not necessarily the ELCA] say that in its pastoral practice, the Church should bless mutually loving, faithful relationships between two gay men or two lesbian women. These relationships are not to be viewed as a "lesser of evils" in a fallen creation. Rather they are an equivalent to marriage and are to be governed by the same norms as heterosexual marriage.

This moral approach is often labeled the "full acceptance" position. While it is not held by many mainline Christian churches as their official position, it has received greater theological support in recent decades and, for many years, has been the official stance of the English Quakers.

Q. 53. But isn't the Bible pretty blunt in its condemnation of homosexual actions? How do these "full acceptance" Christians explain away the biblical witness?

The Bible contains four types of passages related to homosexuality: (1) references to Sodom and Gomorrah (Gen. 19:1–11; Judg. 19:22–30; Matt. 10:15; 11:24; Luke 10:12; 17:29; 2 Pet. 2:6–10; Jude 7); (2) Hebrew legal prohibitions (Lev. 18:22; 20:13; Deut. 23:17); (3) New Testament "sin lists" (1 Cor. 6:9–10; 1 Tim. 1:10); and (4) Paul's exhortation in Rom. 1:24–28. It is beyond the scope of this book and this condensed response to unpack all the scholarly opinions concerning each of these passages. There are biblical literalists, who would lift these negative quotations out of their scriptural context and drop them unnuanced onto the situations of twentieth-century homosexual persons. There are also cultural relativists who would so contextualize these passages within the ancient Hebrew worldview and customs that they lose *any* normative merit for the present situation. Contrary to either polar position, I am persuaded by those scholars who, in doing their homework, struggle to see what these scripture prohibitions meant in context and then to discern what significance they might have for us today, twenty to thirty centuries later.

Despite our use of the term "sodomy" as a synonym for one form of homosexual sex, the sins for which the ancient cities of Sodom and Gomorrah were destroyed are not neatly reduced to homosexual acts. On the eve of Sodom's destruction the mob of townsmen gathered outside Lot's home, demanding that the two male visitors (angels in disguise) be brought out so that they might *know* them ("know" being a biblical euphemism for sexual activity). Yes, their desire seems to be for male/male sex, but it is also an act of rape, since it is involuntary and nonloving. It can also be construed as an act of sacrilege, since the intended victims are holy beings, angels of God.

The situation is further confused by the fact that Lot offers his two daughters to the mob in place of his angelic guests. How could a loving father make such an offer? Numerous scholars point out that among nomadic peoples there was an ancient custom or law of hospitality, whereby even an enemy, seeking shelter from a desert storm, might claim a night's lodging, free of fear for life or limb. If such desert hospitality was Lot's priority, all the more since his guests were divinely sent, then offering his own daughters instead of his guests makes some tragic sense.

It's interesting to note that the only time in the Gospels that Jesus mentions Sodom, it is not in connection with sexual sins, but with a lack of hospitality. He advises his disciples to kick the dust off their sandals from any town that does not welcome them. "Truly I tell you, it will be more tolerable for the land of Sodom and Gomorrah on the day of judgment than for that town" (Matt 10:15). At the very least, the sinful act in the Sodom story is homosexual *rape*, and it may well be more about *sacrilege* or even a gross breach of Hebrew *hospitality*.

The other passages benefit in a similar way from being contextualized. The Old Testament legal prohibitions against lying with a man as with a woman (Lev. 18:22; 20:13; and Deut. 23:17) and the New Testament listing of homosexuality among the sins that prevent one from entering God's kingdom (1 Cor. 6:9–10; 1 Tim. 1:10) are surely clear enough. However, the former find some, not all, of their negative character in ritual purity codes, which similarly declare one "unclean" after menstruation and nocturnal emissions, neither of which was or is considered "immoral." In the same way, Paul's sin lists also contain "drunkards" and "userers" (i.e., those who lend money with interest) as condemned souls. Today we see alcoholism as a disease requiring help, not a moral defect. And bankers and loan officers would be quaking in their boots if we didn't differentiate between rightful interest-taking and immoral loan-sharking. In short, while we ought not to twist these passages around to make homosexuality a virtue, in the transition from then to now they are not absolutely clear prohibitions of all homosexual genital acts.

But one might protest that Paul is being eminently clear when he says:

> For this reason God gave them up to degrading passions. Their women exchanged natural intercourse for unnatural, and in the same way also the men, giving up natural intercourse with women, were consumed with passion for one another. Men committed shameless acts with men and received within their own persons the due penalty for their error. (Rom. 1:26–27)

Some scholars point out that Paul speaks of women and men choosing to "exchange" or "give up" natural intercourse for unnatural. Paul seems to have no awareness of the possibility that one's basic sexual *orientation* might be toward one's own gender, that it is a discovery—whether natural or a fluke of nature—not freely chosen.

In Corinth and other prosperous cities of the Roman empire pederasty (i.e., sex with young boys) was not uncommon and its practitioners seem to have been not homosexual males but happily married heterosexual men who freely chose to "give up" natural intercourse with their wives for sexual exploitation of pubescent boys. This practice would seem to be clearly against their nature, as well as a form of what we would consider today child abuse or pornography. Paul's condemnation of it is on target. But Paul, a first-century Jew, was unaware of genetics, hormones, psychosocial factors, and all that twentieth-century science brings to our discussion of the distinction between discovering one's orientation and choosing to act that out genitally.

So while the scriptures cannot and ought not to be facilely "explained away" on the topic of homosexuality—for they are obviously negative about the subject—once the passages are placed in context, there is at least some room to discuss whether homosexual sex for a committed gay or lesbian couple is absolutely forbidden or might be the exception that proves the usual biblical prohibition of homosexual genital activity. However, once one adds to the scriptural witness the twenty centuries of the church's tradition, then the Christian prohibition of all homosexual sex becomes more definitively held. But on scriptural evidence alone we are left short of a clear and clean condemnation of what might be called committed or covenantal homosexual acts. If you care to read more about these scriptural passages in context, I recommend the scripture sections in either of two books by Gerald Coleman, *Homosexuality: Catholic Teaching and Pastoral Practice* (New York: Paulist Press, 1995) or *Human Sexuality: An All Embracing Gift* (Staten Island: Alba House, 1992).

Q. **54. One last question about homosexuality—would it be morally right or wrong for society to pass legislation guaranteeing homosexual rights?**

In a 1976 pastoral letter, *To Live in Christ Jesus*, the Catholic bishops in this country made it clear that "homosexual [persons], like everyone else, should not suffer from prejudice against their basic human rights. They have the right to respect, friendship, and justice. They should have an active role in the Christian community." This is the basic position of most mainline Christian churches. We're all made in the image and likeness of God, and our human dignity is inherent and abiding. We are worthy of human respect because God made us so, not because we are perfect or have earned it.

Therefore, when it comes to basic human rights—the right to food, shelter, clothing, housing, a job, healthcare, and to be secure in one's core human freedoms—having a homosexual orientation ought not to be grounds for discrimination. In cities and states where so-called gay-rights legislation is proposed, it is morally wrong for Christians to protest with a flat or categorical "No, not in our community." Here some fine lines need to be drawn. For those Christians and other citizens who believe that it is moral for persons with a homosexual orientation to express their love genitally (within certain committed boundaries), laws to protect gay and lesbian people might be achieved by simply adding "homosexual persons" to the list of other groups protected in current civil rights legislation. However, for those Christians and other citizens who acknowledge that a homosexual orientation is not in itself sinful because it is not chosen but who do believe that homosexual sex is immoral, it would be saying too much to simply insert the term "homosexual persons" into civil rights legislation alongside "race, creed, color, or national origin."

What does this mean in terms of public policy and civil law? First, supporting legislation that prohibits discrimination against gay and lesbian people simply for *being* homosexual would seem to be the humane, Christian thing to do. As the United Methodists phrase it, in their 1992 *Book of Discipline*:

> Certain basic human rights and civil liberties are due all persons. We are committed to support those rights and liberties for homosexual persons. We see a clear issue of simple justice in protecting their rightful claims where they have: shared material resources, pensions, guardian relationships, mutual powers of attorney, and other such lawful claims typically attendant to contractual relationships which involve shared contributions, responsibilities, and liabilities, and equal protection before the law. (#71)

However, not all legislation stops at defending a homosexual person's right to *be* who he or she is. Some legislation goes on to promote or at least to accept an environment in which homosexual sex seems to be condoned. Some argue that if it is moral and legal to be gay or lesbian, it is discriminatory to prohibit gay or lesbian people from expressing themselves sexually. Others say we can accept persons as they are—heterosexual, homosexual, or bisexual—but not promote, by law, actions that many believe to be immoral. Still others suggest that bedroom activity ought to be left in the realm of personal morality, one's conscience decision, and not legislated into public policy. As you can see, the legislation question is a delicate one. I suggest that the core issue ought to be promoting universal respect for every person's abiding human dignity. In a pluralistic democracy the process for resolving disputed legal questions ought to be civil discourse with a presumption of good will on the part of all involved.

Q. 55. What do you have to say about masturbation?

The issue of auto-erotic or solitary genital sex is one that requires both moral and pastoral reflection. It has often been a taboo subject, particularly among more puritanical Christian groups. A recent surgeon general of the United States lost her federal job, in part because she suggested we should speak more openly about masturbation in sexuality education programs. Some psychologists today insist that it is such a common practice, especially among adolescents, that we ought to condone it as normal and healthy self-exploration. However, many Christians, including the Catholic church and some mainline Protestant churches, balk at such an easy acceptance of solo sexual orgasms. If, as we noted earlier, genital sexual activity is meant to be an expression of love, an embodied self-gift of one person to another, then obviously sex alone is missing a key element—the partner. So too, if sexual intercourse is in some sense fundamentally linked to the possibility of procreation, sex alone, whether male or female, is missing altogether this procreative potential.

Those who believe that masturbation is morally wrong vary when it comes to judging both the degree of seriousness and the appropriate pastoral response. The Catholic church considers it a seriously immoral action in the objective sphere, but recommends sensitivity and understanding in counseling and educational settings. One's subjective guilt should be evaluated with a measure of prudence and compassion. For example, in the case of adolescents, there are questions related to the teenager's maturity level as well as evolving hormone activity. In the case of persons who have recently lost a spouse through death, divorce, or other long-term separation, these situational factors likely lessen one's moral culpability for compensatory acts of masturbation. Other Christians suggest that such situational elements as age, hormones, loneliness, depression, and marital status impact not only subjective culpability, but the objective moral judgment as well.

Masturbation is often a symptom of underlying personal issues—low self-esteem, loneliness, frustrations in other aspects of one's life, or relational tensions. Focusing on these personal and interpersonal issues frequently is of more help to the person than concentrating on the act itself. With the exception of the few who believe masturbation is psychologically normal and therefore moral, most Christians believe that "sex alone" is less than the ideal, immoral to varying degrees, with pastoral care and sensitivity being the key elements in dealing with it effectively.

Q. 56. It seems as if everywhere you look—film, television, novels, magazines, advertisements—you see human bodies, naked or scantily clad, engaged in sexual behavior or striking provocative poses. What can we do about all this pornography?

First of all, let's attempt to define the term. *Pornography* refers to "the use of visual or print media to present nudity or sexual activity in a degrading or depersonalizing way." Not all nudity or sexual expression in media is pornographic. For example, obviously the nudes on the ceiling of the Sistine Chapel are considered Michelangelo's masterpieces, not pornography. So, too, a sexual scene in a film or a piece of fiction can be tastefully handled, fit within the context of the story, and enhance the viewer's or reader's appreciation of life, love, sensuality, and sexuality. On the other hand, entertainment that is aimed primarily at titillating the prurient interests of the viewer is all too common in our society today. It is doubtful whether playmates-of-the-month or other nudie pinups are being viewed as whole persons. Such portrayals of women as "cheesecake" or men as "hunks" tend to dull our sensitivities to the real persons who are being airbrushed, glamorized, and depersonalized. Such depictions also serve to trivialize sexuality and sex itself.

Sexual harassment, sexual misconduct, and sexual abuse are on the rise in our society. While pornography is not the only cause of such psychologically destructive and immoral actions, it does seem to be a contributing factor. This is an issue that calls for a community-wide response. Writers, artists, actors, producers, directors, distributors, venders, critics, and the wider public need to accept responsibility for what we produce and what we consume in the media market. Sexuality is not and ought not to be a forbidden subject in the arts and media. By working together, we can create communities in which the arts can flourish, free speech can be upheld, and pornography will find no place.

Q. 57. There seems to be so much child abuse going on today and being reported in the news. How should we think about and respond to this? If it's as wrong as I think it is,

why do so many parents, clergy, coaches, and trusted adults seem to do it?

You're right. There is no way that Christianity, rooted as it is in a respect for human dignity and the call to unselfish love, can ever condone the sexual manipulation and use of children for the gratification of an adult. You're also right in noting that often the perpetrator is a "trusted adult," someone who has been entrusted by God, by society, or by others, to be the caretaker and protector of this young person. To abuse this trust is seriously wrong. No amount of rationalization can justify such actions.

That said, as more long-term data accrue from the treatment and aftercare of young victims as well as from the study of therapy for those adults responsible for the molestations, we are coming to realize that personal culpability is often colored by one's own past experiences, one's own psychological and mental state. Adults who themselves were abused as children seem to have a greater potential or propensity to abuse their own children or others of the next generation. *Pedophilia* (i.e., sex with children) and *ephebophilia* (i.e., sex with adolescents) are not new phenomena, but only in recent decades have we begun to do long-range studies on therapies, "cure rates," and how effective recovery might be. So, while there ought to be no tolerance of the sexual abuse of children in the moral or legal spheres, our response as a Christian and humane community should include compassion and therapeutic care especially for the innocent victims but also for the perpetrators, who themselves may be victims in a longer string of events. I hope I'm being clear on this. Sexual abuse of children or other vulnerable persons is objectively, categorically, seriously wrong. This is truly a case for the old adage, "hate the sin, but (as best we can) love the sinner." For indeed, he or she needs psychiatric help and pastoral care far more than moral condemnation. (See also Q. 94 on spousal abuse and domestic violence.)

Q. **58. So where does the Christian tradition stand on sex education—for it or against it?**

First, let's broaden the concept to sexuality education, not solely sex education. There is no single Christian position on this. When and how to teach young people about the sexual dimension of their lives is not primarily a moral question, but one of age appropriateness, teaching methods, and community standards. In the *Declaration on Christian Education* of the Second Vatican Council (1965) we find this statement: "As they [children and young people] advance in years, they should be given positive and prudent sexual education." In some communities sexuality instruction is reserved to the parents in the privacy of their own homes. Parents are entrusted by God, by nature, and by the community to be the primary educators of their own children, in sexuality as in all matters. Just as families seek community assistance in educating their children in other facets of life, so too in this core dimension of life parents well may seek the assistance of their school, church, and civic organizations. There is nothing inherently wrong with formal sexuality education, despite the rather vocal protests of some on the far right of various Christian denominations.

In many communities sexuality education in schools, church religious education programs, and other community settings dates back to the 1950s. Provided that sexual *information* is handled with finesse, age appropriateness, and within the wider context of *formation* in moral values, formal instruction can be a helpful supplement to parental efforts and intra-familial modeling.

> Education in sexuality includes all dimensions of the topic: moral, spiritual, psychological, emotional, and physical. Its goal is training in chastity in accord with the teaching of Christ and the Church. . . . (*Sharing the Light of Faith*, 1977)

 59. While we're on the topic of sexuality education, what do you have to say about feminism and the women's movement? What should we be teaching young women and men of the next generation about their gender identity and roles?

I'm delighted that you asked this question. If you hadn't raised it, I would have. It probably belongs right up there after question 41, as part of our discussion of "sexuality" in general. In her balanced little book *Responses to 101 Questions about Feminism*, Denise Lardner Carmody defines *feminism* as a "commitment to the equality of women and men." She goes on to suggest that men as well as women can be "feminists," provided they are committed to redressing the inequities fostered by centuries-old patterns of male chauvinism and patriarchy. No, this is not intended to demean either sex, nor to reduce some of the rightful differences that exist in anatomy, genetic makeup, hormonal balances, and cultural roles. But the women's movement, grounded as it is in much twentieth-century scholarship and cultural evolution, does call for a fundamental reevaluation of how men and women relate to each other, seeking to root out those patterns of power abuse and domination which are neither inherently human nor divinely ordained. So too, the hope would be that girls and boys of the next generation might grow up with a healthier sense of personal worth and a broader, less stereotyped concept of gender identity and roles.

Some in the feminist movement assert that all distinctions between the sexes are cultural overlays and that we would be not only equal but identical if such cultural programming were removed. Most, however, don't believe such extreme or "radical feminism" is necessary or consistent with the biological, genetic, and psychological data concerning both the human species and other male and female animals. The concept of male/female "complementarity"—mentioned above in terms of the presumed heterosexual norm—is hotly debated today. Pope John Paul II defends it vigorously, while many prefer the term "mutuality," fearing that if one adheres too strongly to the notion that women complete men and vice versa, there will be little impetus to challenge or change assumed sexual roles and long-standing patterns of male domination of women.

Those who are skeptical about feminist concerns and who adopt a more fundamentalistic approach to the Bible tend to rely heavily on Eph. 5:22–23: "Wives, be subject to your husbands as you are to the Lord. For the husband is the head of the wife, just as Christ is the head of the church. . . ." Others, more sympathetic to feminist equality concerns, tend to quote Gal. 3:28 as a counterbalancing passage: "There is no longer Jew or Greek, there is no longer slave or free, there is no longer male or female; for all of you are one in Christ Jesus." Underlying any moral discussion of gender identity and roles must be the firm Christian belief in the inherent, abiding, and equal dignity of all people, women no less than men. But since "equality" does not necessarily mean "being identical," there is room for an honest discussion among Christians, indeed among all people of good will, about what constitutes fairness and a reasonable measure of respect for some valid gender differences.

Obviously, in addition to the complexity of workplace and homemaking concerns, there are intra-church issues related to the role of women within Christian churches and local parish communities or congregations. The issue of women's ordination—resolved by many Protestant churches in a way much different from the Catholic church—is the tip of the moral and institutional iceberg related to women's access to ministerial service and power. Some balk at bringing the issue of "power" into this discussion; however, power is not a dirty word. If God has entrusted us with talents and gifts as well as the freedom to exercise those gifts, then that also involves the necessary power or ability to discern values, to choose, and to act accordingly. That's pretty close to our basic definition of *morality* back in question 1—one's values, choices, and actions. We are in the first phase of a long process of communal moral discernment about the rights and evolving roles of women and men in our culture. This response is only a modest contribution to that ongoing moral discussion. (See also Q. 94 on domestic violence and sexism.)

Q. **60. Do you have a final word on sexual morality before I begin another line of questions?**

Human sexuality is a *wonderful gift* of God and therefore an *awesome responsibility*. Some might suggest "wonderful gift" and "lots of potential for sin." No, while there is surely the potential for sexual misuse and abuse of ourselves and others, I believe Christianity for too long has accentuated the negative rather than the positive. Learning to live morally as sexual beings is a lifelong process. The more and better we can integrate our sexuality into our lives, the greater will be the blessing and the lesser the potential moral harm. Accurate sexuality *information*, taught within the context of Christian and moral *formation*, bodes well for future generations of men and women, boys and girls, whether married or single, straight or gay, old or young, sexually active or celibate.

Chastity, not sexual repression, is our goal—being sexually appropriate and responsible for who we are as embodied sexual persons—men, women, and children of faith. Increasingly our Christian focus is shifting from being overly focused on the morality of specific sex acts to a greater concern for the virtues of healthy human relationships and commitment, including their sexual dimensions. Fidelity, sensitivity, mutuality, good communication, trust, self-sacrifice, and generosity are some of the virtues to be fostered in this broader, fuller approach to sexual morality.

PART FOUR

Issues in Political and Economic Life

Q. **61. What does Christianity have to say about the role or value of government in our lives?**

This is an important question, especially in this era when so many denounce government as if it were the "problem" or the "enemy." Many assume that all or most politicians are corrupt or at least inept, lending credence to the idea that less government is automatically better. The Christian tradition supports neither of these conclusions, at least not in so simplistic a fashion.

In the Hebrew Scriptures there is a tendency to wed religious faith to civil authority because the chosen people saw themselves as ruled directly by God. Thus, when God permitted them to establish judges and eventually kings (e.g., Saul, David, Solomon), Israel was, in effect, a *theocracy*, that is, a state governed by God, under the immediate headship of divinely ordained rulers. The concept of the "divine right of kings," which later bolstered the authority of medieval rulers in Europe, found support in this ancient sense of God electing and empowering earthly monarchs. At the time of the Reformation, Calvin attempted to reinstitute a full-blown theocracy in his Reformed community in Geneva.

In the New Testament we find several passages concerning the relationship of people of faith to civil government, each more deferential in tone than suspicious. When asked about the legitimacy of paying taxes to the emperor, Jesus examined the coin of the realm, noted Caesar's image, and simply replied, "Give to the emperor the things that are the emperor's and to God the things that are God's" (Mark 12:17; Matt. 22:21; Luke 20-25). Clearly, Christians are called to place duty to God before duty to civil authority, but, assuming that God empowers civil authorities for their tasks, we are to respect and submit to their leadership in all pertinent matters. In his letter to the Romans, Paul confirms this call for Christians to be respectful of civil leaders. "Let every person be subject to the governing authorities; for there is no authority except from God, and those authorities which exist have been instituted by God" (Rom. 13:1; cf. Titus 3:1; 1 Pet. 2:13–14).

Given our twentieth-century experiences of Nazism, fascism, and communism, understandably we are more cautious about assuming that civil authorities have divine benediction for all that they decree or do. Moreover, those who live in democratic societies believe that if civil authority does receive divine approbation, it is *through the consent of the governed*, not directly from God's throne. The divine right of kings has been replaced by a greater trust that God works through the will of the people in open debate, free elections, and constitutional forms of governance.

Q. **62. If the government is to be treated neither as the enemy nor as directly appointed by God, how are we to view civil officials, the state, and the law of the land?**

Mainline Christianity, as exemplified in the writings of Thomas Aquinas, speaks of government as a natural good, a tool or vehicle designed to promote the "common good." The common good is *not* a synonym for the good of the majority over against individual rights and liberty, though often it is misunderstood that way. Rather, the notion of the *common good* attempts to hold in creative tension the best interest of each individual with the well-being of the community as a whole. One way of saying that is that *the good of all is tied up in respecting the inherent and abiding dignity of each individual person or member of the community.*

Thus, in the best of societies, there is special provision made for those weaker members of the community who cannot provide for themselves—persons with physical or mental disabilities, the unemployed, needy children, and those chronically ill, aged, or infirm. Taking care of our poor and those in need is *not* seen as a matter of *charity*, that is, nice to do but not obligatory. Rather, it is viewed as a matter of *justice*. If we, and the governments we elect, are in some sense empowered by God to act in worldly affairs, then our response must bespeak our Christian values. The people in general, our corporate and business enterprises, and our governments are all involved in the God-given task of making a given community more civilized, more like the "reign of God," which Jesus came to proclaim. So, to answer your question, if civil officials serve the community wisely and well, we owe them our vote of confidence, our cooperation, and our gratitude.

At the very least, good government promotes *public order*, a modicum of peace and justice, a basically humane environment, in which individuals, families, and small communities can flourish and grow. Laws and their enforcement are designed to foster this wholesome environment. We do not attempt in civil statutes either to prescribe or mandate every kind of behavior that we think is morally ideal nor to proscribe or prohibit every action we think is immoral. The most heinous of immoral actions—murder, rape, spouse and child abuse, blatant racism, embezzlement, bribery— these are outlawed and strictly enforced. However, other moral issues, which are either too personal for government oversight or about which there is no clear moral consensus, remain in the realm of personal moral discernment rather than civil statutes. In deciding whether to enact a given civil law, we try to evaluate it for equitability, enforceability, and whether it allows some room for situational common sense and prudent application by the police, the courts, and the individuals involved.

Q. **63. In the best of societies that all may be true, but what is a Christian citizen to do in a country where public officials are corrupt or, at best, inept?**

I confess to being ill-at-ease with the current cultural climate that tends to assume that *all* public officials—whether local, regional, or federal—are corrupt or inept. I think there is a kind of herd mentality afoot which caricatures public officials as if they were all cigar-chomping, backroom-dealing, on-the-take crooks. This simply is not true. While politics, like every other arena of life, has its share of blatantly corrupt people, and while none of us, including politicians, is ever perfect or completely sin-free, it seems unfair to assume that every person who offers his or her service to the community is doing so for base or ulterior motives. Some "public servants" are truly that, people seeking to serve the good of the community.

In addition, it is our responsibility as citizens to participate in civic matters, to discern and to vote wisely. Too often in election campaigns people are swayed by "sound bites" that smear the opposing candidate with half-truths and unfounded accusations. Polls indicate that more often than not we tend to vote our personal pocketbooks, with too little concern for the welfare of others. As we noted earlier, a community that is truly humane and Christian ought to focus more on the common good than on "what's in it for me." That's as true for us as individual citizens as it is for our elected officials and for those doing business or practicing their professions in our communities.

Mindful of the fact that all authority originates with God, and yet prudent enough to know that not all elected or appointed leaders exercise their authority with sufficient virtue and grace, I think the Christian citizen is called (1) to respect public office always, (2) to strive to respect and support those in office as much as possible, and (3) to remain active and vigilant participants in the ongoing electoral process. At times, one may be called to raise a prophetic or dissenting voice, even to the point of an act of civil disobedience (see Q. 87), always centered on the common good of each and all. Know too that the private sector and business community have responsibilities as well. Many of our personal and communal concerns revolve around the economy, over which government has only limited control and authority.

Q. 64. Then is there one preferred Christian economic system?

No, the various Christian churches do not baptize any one economic system, as if God were a free-market capitalist or a card-carrying socialist or a devotee of the feudal guild system. While at various times in history churches have aligned themselves too uncritically with certain political and economic regimes, at best Christianity adopts no single economic or political system as if it were divinely ordained. In every age Christian denominations—through councils, synods, hierarchies, presbyteries, boards of elders, congregations, and national or regional conferences—try to apply timeless gospel values when evaluating contemporary economic theories and political movements.

In the late nineteenth century it was Leo XIII who defended the right of factory workers and laborers to unite, to form unions, and to bargain collectively for fair wages, decent working conditions, and benefits for their families. In an era when such talk usually branded one as a Marxist, an aristocratic Italian pope stepped forward to uphold that the mutual rights and duties of labor and management are rooted in gospel values, not solely the purview of one economic philosophy. During the two world wars of this century, it was Christians such as Lutheran Dietrich Bonhoeffer who stood up as prophets and peacemakers, opposing the tyranny and genocide perpetrated by fascist regimes. Bonhoeffer knew well "the cost of discipleship" and, like Christ, paid it in full, executed in a Nazi prison. And in the last two decades, it has been Christian leaders like John Paul II, Lech Walesa, and Vaclav Havel who passionately defended the rights of workers in Poland, Czechoslovakia, and other Eastern bloc countries, urging them to stand in *solidarity* for their basic God-given human, political, and economic rights.

Ideally, in each era Christianity brings the lens of the gospel to bear on the economic, political, and social issues of the day, seeking a more humane and Christ-like civil community. Christians approach all economic and political systems with the two-edged sword of the gospel. "Indeed, the word of God is living and active, sharper than any two-edged sword, piercing until it divides soul from spirit, joints from marrow; it is able to judge the thoughts and intentions of the heart" (Heb. 4:12). Endorsing no system uncritically, Christian leaders and people strive to praise whatever is virtuous and promotes human dignity and the common good, while criticizing and challenging that which is counterproductive and contrary to basic human rights and social well-being.

Q. **65. But surely wouldn't you agree that God approves more of capitalism than socialism?**

Let me answer this question carefully. There is both an "in theory" response and an "in practice" one, and the two are not the same. In theory, one might argue that capitalism, in its purest, laissez-faire form, bespeaks a "survival of the fittest" mentality, sort of an economic Darwinism, in which the shrewdest entrepreneur will win, the least competitive will lose, and along the way *caveat emptor* (i.e., let the buyer beware). At that level one could hardly call it the Christian way. So too, one might suggest that in theory socialism sounds a lot more like the ideal Christian community as described in the Acts of the Apostles: "Now the whole group of those who believed were of one heart and soul, and no one claimed private ownership of any possessions, but everything they owned was held in common" (Acts 4:32).

But in practice one must stir into that mix the reality of original sin. In this post-Soviet era one finds some pro-capitalist theologians who argue in favor of the free-market system as if it were divinely ordained, the closest thing to God's kingdom come. I believe it is truer to suggest that, given human sinfulness, an economic system that is predominantly capitalist or free-market-oriented better takes into account our human need for reward and punishment. The "carrots" of profits, promotions, and success as well as the "sticks" of debts, demotion, and potential job loss seem to encourage or goad us as individuals and groups into greater productivity and effort. If it were not for human sinfulness (e.g., selfishness, greed, sloth, envy), the socialist approach, in which everyone produces to one's maximum capacity while receiving relatively the same share of the profits, would be no problem. We would give our best, while echoing the gospel response, "We are worthless slaves [servants]; we have done only what we ought to have done" (Luke 17:10).

Unfortunately, humans crave a bit more praise for a job well done and are usually encouraged along by the benign threat of losing some benefit if they fail to perform well. Thus, a basic free-market economy would seem to better acknowledge the reality of post-Eden human nature, while the socialist system somewhat naïvely tends to underestimate human sinfulness, our propensity to need rewards and to avoid hardship. Add to this the harsh historical incarnations of communist socialism in this century—the fact that socialism too often has been tied to dictatorial political regimes with decidedly materialistic and atheistic philosophies—and one can see why most Christian denominations tilt toward a more free-market approach to economics.

Still, in order for capitalism to pass the Christian litmus test, it must forgo its more laissez-faire or unbridled versions, building in some reasonable and humane checks and balances. Some speak of "an economic safety net," the necessary social services and programs that forestall or correct some of capitalism's harsher results. Others admit that this hybrid form of a free-market economy with some measure of arguably socialist correctives might better be designated "the modern welfare state."

At the same time, it is the special task of Christians to uphold the rights and dignity of those who lack the physical, mental, or financial ability to compete in the marketplace or workforce and those who invested and lost all, those left destitute following a failed economic venture. Like Jesus, we are called to have a certain bias or preferential option on behalf of the poor and those ill-equipped or unable to compete. In effect, Christians ask three core questions in evaluating any economic system or enterprise: (1) Positively speaking, what does it do *for* people? (2) Negatively speaking, what does it do *to* people? (3) And how are people empowered to *participate* in the economic enterprise? By responding to these three questions one gets some glimpse of the human and moral impact of a given economic system or endeavor. By tempering capitalism's competitive spirit with a degree of compassion and social justice, we create an economic system with a bit more heart and humanity.

Q. **66. When we move from the overall economic system to actually doing business, should the gospel take a backseat to the "law of the marketplace"?**

No, I don't think we can park our Christian faith in church on Sunday and live the rest of the week gospel-free. A teacher once said that Christians ought to face each new day with a copy of the Bible in one hand and that day's issue of the *New York Times* in the other. By this he meant that how we live our daily lives—in business as well as in our personal relationships—bespeaks who we are and whether we truly believe in Christ and his message. Remember our early discussion of the relationship between "being" and "doing." Who we are deep down spills over into what we choose to do in life, and what we do, over time, makes us into who we are, whether people of virtue or of vice. As the letter of James attests: "What good is it, my brothers and sisters, if you say you have faith but do not have works? . . . But someone will say, 'You have faith and I have works.' Show me your faith apart from your works, and I by my works will show you my faith" (Jas. 2:14, 18).

Now in terms of one's daily business ventures, being a person of integrity, honest and fair in one's dealings, does not necessarily guarantee maximum financial profit. Often those more shrewd in the ways of financial dealings, and misdealings, profit more in the short run. But it is intriguing to study the sociological research that indicates that morality often pays off, not only in terms of pleasing God and creating an inner sense of integrity, but in long-term profits and business stability as well. Books such as *In Search of Excellence* by Thomas Peters and Robert Waterman (New York: Harper & Row, 1982) and, more recently, Stephen Covey's *Seven Habits of Highly Effective People* (New York: Simon & Schuster, 1989), affirm that those corporations and business leaders who treat customers, employees, and stockholders fairly will remain reasonably profitable and will survive as respected business enterprises *over the long haul*. In the short run, crime or shady business dealings too often do seem to pay. But, in the long run, those who conduct their business affairs with honor earn the community's respect as well as a reasonable return on their investment. In a very real sense, good ethics is good business.

Another way of phrasing this is that there are more *stakeholders* in any business enterprise than just the *stockholders*. If a business puts out a decent product at a fair price for its customers, treats its labor and management employees equitably, garners a reasonable profit for the stockholders, while striving to keep the environment clean and contributing time and talent to community affairs, this business will have served the *common good* of everyone it touches. By envisioning one's business as broader than the bottom line, entrepreneurs and corporations can be better partners with government and the private sector in building and fostering safer, healthier, more productive communities. The move from *being* honest in one's heart to *doing* business honestly requires prudence, planning, wise counsel, and courage. At times one may have to stand alone, especially if one's colleagues are entrenched in business as usual or *caveat-emptor* values.

Q. **67. But shouldn't government keep its nose out of business affairs and out of our personal lives?**

If you're asking whether it's wrong for government to be the first line of defense, the arbiter of all business, family, and personal affairs, you're right. Government is not the first resort, but in some sense the final resort. The term for this tiered approach concerning the role of government is the principle of *subsidiarity*. Wherever possible, personal and interpersonal disputes ought to be handled one to one, between spouses or friends within the family context. So too, most business disputes will be resolved through healthy competition, legal contracts, and market forces such as the law of supply and demand. Christianity is about living our personal and business lives as responsible people of faith, as children of God striving to live as brothers and sisters in our various communities. However, government has a rightful and vital role in this process. At the very least, as noted above, governments guarantee public order. Police and fire protection, safe power and water supplies, schools, interstate highways, and roads are some of the community-wide services that we expect governments to provide.

According to the principle of subsidiarity, governmental services ought, whenever possible, to be handled at the lowest, least intrusive level. Thus, school systems tend to be operated at the local level, under the supervision of district or municipal school boards, funded by local property taxes, bonds, or millage. So too, many social services are handled by one's township or county, and there has been a recent trend, whether for good or ill, to return more control over welfare, food stamps, and Medicaid programs to the individual states. But some public services require larger sums of money or greater intercommunity coordination, for example, maintenance of national highways, interstate and international commerce, military defense, protection of constitutionally guaranteed rights, and preservation of the environment, national parks, and natural resources. For these services the private sector often must rely on government, and quite often state or federal coordination supersedes local or regional abilities and resources. So too, governments intervene to regulate or restructure when private corporations or individuals monopolize an industry, threatening the health, rights, and well-being of innocent people or the community as a whole.

The principle of subsidiarity is not opposed to involvement of the federal government or even the inclusion of international organizations such as the United Nations or the International Monetary Fund, where such national or global efforts are required to protect human dignity and the common good. It is a rule of thumb, however, to strive to deal more efficiently and fairly with issues at the personal or private level first. Then we can involve government, as needed, at the lowest, most local level to meet the community's real needs justly and with sufficient dispatch. Thus, the private sector, through a series of voluntary projects sponsored by churches, community organizations, and even civic-minded businesses, meets many of the social needs of a given municipality or region. Local, county, state, and federal governments step in either when greater coordination or resources are required or if a given basic human need "falls between the cracks" and is not being met by the voluntary efforts of the community. Government at all levels is only one actor, a partner in a multifaceted societal endeavor.

Q. **68. What about issues of justice and fairness? Whose responsibility is it to promote and guarantee justice?**

Let's start by defining and unpacking the notion of *justice* itself. Mainline Christians view *justice* as a wonderfully nuanced and multifaceted virtue. Synonyms include fairness, equity, and rightful respect. Justice is defined as *rendering someone his or her due.* But by what measure do we decide that you are due or owed something? There are at least three different responses to that, all of them valid, each representing a different angle or dimension of the one virtue of *justice,* including (1) *commutative justice,* (2) *distributive justice,* and (3) *social justice.* Each differs in the criteria for determining "fairness," how to measure what is "one's due."

The term *commutative justice* applies to one-to-one contracts, business deals or agreements between individuals, corporate entities, or even nations that are on equal footing. This is the world of 50–50 agreements, where one's due is based on whether one "earns" his or her share. If you do your half of the contract, you have "earned" and are owed whatever compensation we have agreed on. So too, if you deliver the product ordered on time, you have "earned" and are owed the agreed-upon price or commission. Likewise, international treaties are negotiated on an "earned" benefit basis. When two people or businesses or states can act on a level playing field, *commutative justice* says we must earn what is our due by our own efforts and mutual agreements.

However, when we look at what the society as a whole might owe to an individual member of that community, then our focus shifts to the basic "need" of the recipient, not whether she or he can earn society's beneficence. For example, those persons who are physically or mentally disabled may not be able to compete in the marketplace of free enterprise. Their disabilities may be so great that they require protection or assistance from the wider community. We do not provide special education programs, ramps or buses with lifts, and handicap-accessible restrooms because these persons "earned" them. We say that persons who are disabled deserve special attention; it is their "due" based on the *distributive justice* criterion of basic human "need." They deserve our assistance *not* as a matter of charity (i.e., a well-meaning handout) but because it is their due as needy members of a human and humane community. Justice—that is, *distributive justice*—affirms that we owe assistance, the proverbial bootstraps, to those who, through no fault of their own, are unable to compete on a level playing field.

Finally, on what basis do we say that individuals owe something to their community, whether it be taxes, military service, or jury duty? The community has a right to expect from its members according to each one's "ability" to contribute. The graduated income tax system, which has been the law of the land for over a half century now, is based on the *social justice* premise that those with greater income, especially if they have fewer dependents, ought to contribute a larger percentage or dollar amount to the common till. So too, professionals in the field of medicine, law, and accounting are expected to do a certain amount of *pro bono* work for those in need. Free medical clinics, legal aid, and many social services rely on the anticipated voluntarism of persons with time, talent, and treasure to share. This is a matter not solely of charity, of magnanimous self-sacrifice but of *social justice*, an obligation based on one's "ability" to contribute to those in need and to the wider society. Sometimes in the tradition this same dimension or kind of justice has been called *general* or *legal justice*. The gospel of Jesus suggests that from the one who has been given much, much is to be expected.

Q. **69. What about "preferential affirmative action"? Is this attempted cure really another form of unjust discrimination?**

That is a hotly debated question in our society today. Does the attempt to correct past discrimination by instituting a hiring or promotion system that favors ethnic, racial, or gender minorities constitute a new species of bias? Do white, middle-class males suffer a social injustice at the hands of government, employers, and schools that give preferential treatment to people of color, the poor, women, or other minorities? I balk at a simple yes-or-no answer because the issue is complicated by which dimension or angle of justice one stresses.

People in our society who are more pro-business and pro–free enterprise (i.e., conservative Republicans and Libertarians) tend most often to emphasize *commutative justice*, denouncing as "unjust" any benefit that isn't "earned" via healthy competition. Nothing is due someone if they haven't personally "earned" it. Conservative talk-show hosts take this approach to justice all the time and do not consider that justice has two other important dimensions.

By contrast, a liberal Democrat would tend to respond according to *distributive justice*, using the language of fairness versus injustice. According to this perspective, persons of color, certain ethnic minorities, and women in general are to be viewed somewhat like persons with disabilities. Decade after decade of white and male prejudice has stacked professional, economic, and educational systems in their favor. The "good old boy" network has kept others off the playing field for so long that those who have been excluded "need" a break, a *distributive justice* advantage. They need a leg up, an opportunity to attend certain schools and to enter certain professions, a just and fair chance to prove themselves. If the playing field is leveled through "preferential affirmative action" for a given number of applicants or a certain span of time, the competition of *commutative justice* can commence more fairly.

No one that I know suggests that unqualified people ought to be given preferential treatment, and few suggest that rigid quotas or token hirings are the solution to racial, ethnic, or gender inequities. Rather, those who advocate some form of preferential affirmative action suggest that, all things being equal, some points or degree of advantage ought to be given to qualified minorities in order to bring them into the mainstream of professional, business, and educational opportunity.

But, in the short run, does someone else lose out? Does the equally qualified white male applicant have to pay the price for a larger social injustice, over which he had no personal control? For example, is it fair to ask a white male medical school applicant of the 1990s to lose his place because of the racial and gender prejudice of medical schools and doctors in the 1930s, 1940s, and 1950s? Do two wrongs, or potentially two species of injustice, make a right? I have no neat and tidy Christian response. What seem to be at odds here are two different slants on one's just "due," *commutative justice* (what one earns) versus *distributive justice* (what one needs), with those who "lose" being asked, in *social justice* terms (ability), to pay the price. This seems to be built on the assumption that those white male applicants who are passed over have the "ability" to find other avenues of access or other equally rewarding career opportunities.

I believe that those who inaugurated preferential affirmative action had the right intention, but perhaps it was and is not the most equitable solution to correct a long-standing "social sin" in our midst. So, as long as we acknowledge that racism, ethnic bias, and sexism are a negative part of our heritage and still exist in our societal ethos, and as long as we seek alternative ways to redress this grievance against justice, then perhaps we could begin to shift from preferential affirmative action programs to some other societal means to foster access for equally qualified minority applicants. Hopefully such solutions would more equitably distribute the burdens and cost of change, but we must still be cautious in discussions about dismantling or refining our present preferential affirmative action policies.

Justice is a complex and multifaceted reality. One's due may be based on (1) what one "earns," (2) whether one has a basic human "need" (not merely a wish or desire) that she or he cannot fulfill, and (3) whether one has the "ability," the God-given talent or trea-

sure, to contribute to the common good. When we say that something is "unfair" or "unjust," we should pause to ask, By what criteria are we measuring someone's *due?*

Q. **70. You mentioned basic human "need" versus a "wish" or
"desire." Given that the term "human rights" is bandied
about so easily, what does the gospel or Christianity have
to say about human rights?**

Discussion of basic human rights comes to us more from the
Enlightenment philosophy of thinkers like Thomas Hobbes, Jean-
Jacques Rousseau, and John Locke than from the Christian tradition. Still, a number of churches have adopted the language of
human rights to express our core Christian beliefs in (1) the inherent and abiding dignity of humanity, and in (2) our call to live in solidarity, (3) as stewards of creation, (4) fostering the common good.
Human rights, then, can be defined as *those conditions and "things"
necessary to protect and promote basic human dignity in a given society or
community.*

In 1963, shortly before his death, Pope John XXIII issued an
encyclical letter entitled *Peace on Earth,* written to "all people of
good will." In it he outlined two distinct but related sets of human
rights. Most democratically constituted nations understood and
applauded his defense of basic *political rights*—the right to freedom
of thought and speech, freedom of religion, freedom to choose
one's state of life, the right to free assembly and to organize to
redress grievances. However, some were taken aback by John
XXIII's inclusion of a list of basic *economic rights.* Citizens have certain inalienable economic or financial rights—the right to work and
to do so without undue coercion, the right to a just wage (defined as
the amount needed to decently provide for oneself and family), the
right to own private property (within the strictures of one's social
duty and the common good), and the right to some share in the
goods one produces (e.g., corporate profit-sharing). These rights,
along with the basic rights to food, clothing, shelter, rest, medical
care, necessary social services, and education, all carry a financial
as well as a political price tag.

By the same token, many people today confuse basic human

needs, the inalienable rights to participate in the goods of life, with personal wishes, wants, or desires. Just because a person wants something—a new car, a better job, fancier or greater material possessions, or unlimited access to healthcare or other finite resources—does not mean he or she has a "right" to it. Nor are others obliged to give or assist someone in securing all their earthly desires or wishes. Rights involve corresponding duties. If someone has a right to something, then either that person or others in the community are obliged, all things being equal, to provide that person with his or her due. To the extent that a society and its economy are not in depression or on the brink of collapse, that community has a responsibility to ensure that basic economic rights (i.e., needs) be met.

Whenever possible, one satisfies these fundamental human needs by *earning* their fulfillment, by contributing to the productivity of the community. *Commutative justice* demands this as only fair and just. At the same time, provided the society is solvent and able, certain needs will be provided for by the community, based solely on the unmet human *need* of the petitioners. Thus, universal access to public schools, to the court system, to police protection, and to a modicum of social services is deemed just and fair for all, an expression of *distributive justice*. And the costs are to be born equitably by the whole community, through voluntarism and taxation, from each member according to his or her *ability* to contribute (i.e., *social justice*).

Q. **71. Does a person really have a right to a job? Isn't "work" one of the flexible variables in the economic equation?**

The most honest Christian response is yes and no. Certainly the labor component is one of the key factors an owner must figure in when calculating the cost of production. Raw material is another piece of the economic equation. The difference, however, is that raw material is inanimate—wood, metal, stone, plastic, chemical, fiber, or whatever—while labor is human and alive. Work or human labor is something *more* than a commodity to be marketed in the economic cycle or chain. Yes, in a sense, we "sell" or "barter" our labor in exchange for salaries and benefits. But labor is not solely a commodity. One's work bespeaks the inner person and involves one's sense of self, one's ability to participate in something creative, and ultimately one's contribution to personal and communal well-being.

Pope John Paul II's encyclical *On Human Labor* (1981) is an eloquent Christian reflection on the dignity and meaning of work. All work has a threefold moral significance. First, it is the primary way humans have to express themselves as creative beings. Second, it is the ordinary means for people to fulfill their own material needs. If one is the breadwinner for a family, then that whole family unit depends on this person's ability to earn a living wage, to "bring home the bacon." Third, work enables one to make his or her mark, to contribute in some way to the well-being of the larger community. Whether we work in a factory or on a farm, in sales or in one of the professions, whether we are part of labor or management, having a job says that we are needed and that what we do matters.

I know that we should appreciate a person for who he or she is, not solely for what they produce. Each of us has an abiding human dignity, regardless of our production capacity or lack thereof. But what we do, what we accomplish with our time and talent, in some sense does affirm our value and worth. It says that we are a contributing member of this community and our contribution is recognized—by salary, by benefits, by promotions, by positive performance reviews, and by the very fact that our employer continues to keep us on the job.

Loss of one's job impacts the individual as a whole person—physically, psychologically, socially, and spiritually. There is ample evidence that being unemployed has devastating effects on most people and on their families and wider social network. Alcoholism, marital problems, divorce, spouse and child abuse, depression, and suicide occur more frequently in families struggling with recent unemployment or long-term work-related disability.

So, does someone else automatically owe us a job? Of course not. All things being equal, we are to develop our talents and skills and offer them in the marketplace. However, it is the goal of a healthy economy and a humane society to achieve "full employment," a job with a living wage for every person who needs and seeks such work. If a nation is in an economic recession or depression, then full employment is an impossibility. But provided the economy is strong or growing, it is incumbent on the private sector, with government incentives or actual participation, to create new and better jobs for those seeking gainful employment.

Whatever the state of the economy, employers must always be cognizant of the fact that cutting labor costs affects human lives deeply. Although personnel departments are often called "human resource" departments today, the emphasis must remain on *human*. Workers are not solely a *"resource,"* akin to raw material. Downsizing, cutting labor costs, permanently eliminating positions—these are the current euphemisms for firing people, putting them out of work. We ought never to lose sight of the faces and lives of those affected by labor decisions. Yes, work is one variable in the economic equation, but it is also so much more.

Q. **72. Do you think that the poor on welfare take advantage of the government? Is it Christian for them to abuse our generosity or for us to foster dependence by keeping people "on the dole" year after year?**

This is a commonly heard complaint in our society, especially around tax time and when elections are near. In approaching this question Christians would do well to remember two wise sayings of Jesus: "Let anyone among you who is without sin be the first to throw a stone" (John 8:7); and "You hypocrite, first take the log out of your own eye, and then you will see clearly to take the speck out of your neighbor's eye" (Matt. 7:5). These two quotations serve as a caution, reminding us not to judge too harshly the financial "sins" of *some* of the people on welfare, without also acknowledging our own indiscretions regarding work responsibilities, money, taxes, and contributions (or lack thereof) to charity and those in need. The Wall Street traders who made millions on insider information, the business moguls who raided corporate pension funds, and those financiers who caused the savings-and-loan scandal of the 1980s are each guilty of far more grievous thefts from the community than those who finagle surplus food stamp booklets or an extra AFDC (Aid to Families with Dependent Children) check here and there.

It is easy for people who are gainfully employed or financially solvent to point a finger at those who are unemployed or homeless and assume that they are *all* boondogglers and welfare cheats. Anecdotes abound about people on welfare who supposedly bilked the government out of huge sums of money through elaborate welfare and food-stamp fraud. When traced to their source, most of these stories turn out to be apocryphal or grossly exaggerated. I am in no way defending people who cheat others, whether the victim is the government or the general public. Nor do I want to perpetuate a social welfare system that, in some cases, might invite people to stay on the public dole because those minimum wage jobs available to them don't pay a living wage. But I do caution against argument by unsubstantiated anecdote and wrathful judgment by armchair critics who lack the facts.

The recession of the 1980s led many companies to cut their work force significantly. Many blue-collar and white-collar workers whose jobs were permanently lost came to realize, perhaps for the first time, that one could be unemployed, poor, and in need *through no fault of their own.* Tragically, many who had worked dutifully for decades were out of work and in financial need because of market forces beyond their control. Welfare as we know it was inaugurated during the Great Depression of the 1930s. For the first time in history, the government stepped in to provide educational opportunities, jobs, job training, and, where necessary, direct financial aid to those left homeless or unemployed in the aftermath of the Crash of 1929. Because the problem was a social one, a systemic downturn in the free-market economy, society, through its government as well as voluntary agencies, felt obliged to help. Feeding the hungry, housing the homeless, and, where possible, assisting people to get back to work seemed to be the civic-minded and humane things to do.

However, as we view our present welfare system some sixty years after the New Deal, most people agree that we've created a giant bureaucracy that needs to be reformed. Like *Uncle Tom's* Topsy, "it just grew" and is now exorbitantly expensive, cumbersome, and often inefficient. Those who truly need the help are stigmatized unfairly by association with the minority of applicants who manipulate the system for personal profit. One popular proposal suggests that people be allowed to stay on welfare a maximum of two years. But at the end of two years if those individuals are not employed, do we let them starve in the street? What about their children? Should children be made to suffer because their parents don't or can't find work? Do we put the children in orphanages and their parents in jail? How much will that cost in the short and long run?

Correcting our present welfare system might require greater sums of money initially—for job training, job placement, and interim child care—with the eventual hope of ending the welfare cycle for some individuals and families. At a time when people scream for balanced budgets and tax relief, are we willing to make the financial investment that true welfare reform may require? Furthermore, certain racial or ethnic groups who already experience prejudice and roadblocks to their entering fully into the economic life of society are often further criticized because they constitute a substantial percentage of those on welfare. Some of our societal backlash may be tinged by racism or ethnic bias.

Complaining about those who cheat or about the size of the welfare system in general is easy. But doing our homework and then making the step-by-step, probably costly changes necessary to fix or reconstruct our social safety net require a commitment beyond armchair complaints. You're right. Fostering long-term dependency on government handouts is not good for anyone. Talk is cheap. True reform is not. Do we have the will, the patience, the humility, and the financial acumen to reform today's welfare system for a leaner, but hopefully *not* a meaner future?

Q. 73. Do we have any financial obligation to assist the poor in other parts of the world?

I'm glad you asked that question. It shows that you realize that the challenge to live as Christians doesn't stop with one's family, ethnic community, or at one's national borders. When Jesus challenged his disciples "to love your neighbor as yourself," he was asked, "And who is my neighbor?" (Luke 10:27, 29). He then recounted the story of the Good Samaritan, who bandaged the wounds of the stranger who had fallen into the hands of robbers. He carried him on his own beast of burden to an inn and paid for his care. Apparently anyone in need is our neighbor.

This does not mean that the countries of the so-called second world (i.e., eastern Europe) or the third world (i.e., emerging nations of Africa, Asia, and the Americas) have a right to receive unlimited, ongoing foreign aid from the first-world nations of the northern and western hemispheres. But it does mean that we are in this global village together. Modern communication and transportation—the information superhighway— have brought us together into an interdependent global economy. The rise and fall of business, currency, the stock market, and trade in one part of the world have ripple effects across national and continental boundaries.

There are few easy answers, but those of us who consume a disproportionate percentage of the world's goods must share the wealth. Pitting first-world labor against cheaper labor in less developed countries is not the long-term solution, either for their industrialization or for our labor force. International trade wars and barriers also seem to ill serve long-term stability. The World Bank, United Nations, International Monetary Fund, and similar worldwide organizations may serve as the vehicles through which nations and corporations can discern together how to facilitate a healthy, prosperous, and just international order.

Personal contributions to international food banks and other relief agencies are certainly good and right. Where necessary, using N.A.T.O., the United Nations, or our own military capabilities to facilitate such relief efforts may be the humanitarian thing to do (e.g., Somalia, Rwanda, Bosnia). However, bandaid efforts amidst drought, famine, or other natural disasters are not permanent solutions to global inequities. In any discussion of economic and political rights, of healthcare access and reform, and of justice, we may start by seeking solutions at home, but our vision must be increasingly global, not national. Am I my brother's and sister's keeper? Yes, and my sisters and brothers are not limited to family or friends. We are all children of God, one family—white, yellow, red, black, and brown. We are called to love one another, to care for one another's needs, and to build, as best we can, the kingdom or reign of God here on planet earth.

Q. **74. Speaking of multiracial cultures, are racism and civil rights arenas where government inevitably must step in?**

This is a good example of a moral issue that often requires government intervention, frequently at the federal level, particularly if a bias or prejudice is deeply rooted in a local community. The United Methodist *Book of Discipline* (1992) defines *racism* as "the combination of the power to dominate by one race over other races and a value system which assumes that the dominant race is innately superior to the others. Racism includes both personal and institutional racism" ("Social Principles," #72).

Prior to the civil rights struggles of the 1950s and 1960s, the idea that black people were somehow inferior, subhuman, and not worthy of equal dignity and respect found deep and broad acceptance across the United States. Although it may have been more entrenched and institutionalized in the deep South (whites-only restaurants, hotels, buses, and drinking fountains), racism and its cousin, ethnic prejudice, color the history of this country north and south, east and west. When local police officials and eventually elected state governors opposed integration and the exercise of constitutionally guaranteed freedoms, the principle of subsidiarity justified moving to the next higher level of authority, the federal government, to secure public order and to defend the basic human and civil rights of minorities. The good of all is tied up in respecting the dignity and rights of every member of the community, especially those weakest, least respected, or most in need.

But my moral concern about racism and ethnic hatred is far more fundamental than a discussion of whether the principle of subsidiarity applies. I worry that deep-seated racial and ethnic hatred has been a sleeping giant, anesthetized for a time by civil rights laws in the West and Soviet domination in the East. Now it is beginning to reawaken worldwide after a half century of relative dormancy. The emergence of white supremacist groups in North America and Europe, the ancient religious and racial hatreds erupting in war and "ethnic cleansing" in Bosnia and eastern Europe, the tribal genocide in African nations such as Rwanda, and the barely hidden Asian versus Anglo mistrust that dominates international commerce—all bespeak an ancient, deeply rooted human tendency to cling to what is familiar while condemning those who are different. The fragile birth of democracy in South Africa and the overthrow of apartheid offer some faint hope for peaceful solutions to these age-old tensions and hostilities. However, I think we each must look more deeply at our own lives, loves, and biases in an effort better to practice what we preach. Jesus reached out to the Samaritans, to women, to the Romans, to public sinners, to the "outcasts" of his day, calling them sisters and brothers. Can we, dare we, do any less? Racism, ethnic bias, sexism, and religiously based prejudice are all "social sins," infecting communities as well as individual hearts. As the American civil rights movement and the South African dismantling of apartheid attest, social ills require collective consciousness raising, systemic change, and social resolve as well as long-term vigilance.

Q. **75. What do you mean by "social sin"? Who is responsible for it? Who will pay the price for it?**

Social sin is the name given to those immoral actions, structures, and ways of thinking that become deeply rooted in the psyche or value system of a given community. Yes, each member of the community is responsible for his or her own bigotry, prejudice, and sinful attitudes. But it seems that succeeding generations would bear less personal responsibility for attitudes modeled and taught by all in that child's world. For example, if everyone uses racial epithets and ethnic slurs, then children will use them without realizing that they are wrong. Such bias is truly "prejudice," a pre-judgment based on societal presumption rather than on one's personal experience or fact. Mandating by law that people of color must sit in the back of the bus, or live in segregated, inferior ghettos or "townships," or be denied their civil right to vote systematizes racism in social structures. Rooting it out will be more difficult than a mere one-to-one call to repentance and conversion.

Christian leaders like John Paul II have cautioned us not to assume that because an evil has become socially acceptable, systematized in one's society or culture, we are no longer personally culpable for it. The leaders of such communities certainly bear the brunt of the responsibility for correcting their community's vision and structures. So too, parents, educators, and business owners share a larger measure of guilt for fostering such attitudes or responsibility for rooting them out In fact, all citizens bear some degree of guilt for any evil that we allow to become embedded in our midst, either by our neglect or by our elective choices. The fact that an evil or sin may become social and systemic does not absolve individuals of the responsibility to change such attitudes and to overturn structures that perpetuate injustice within and beyond one's community.

Q. 76. What about environmental ethics? Is there a Christian position on matters of ecology and the environment?

You can probably guess that I'm going to go to the creation story in Genesis. At the end of the sixth day of creation God blessed the man and the woman and said: "Be fruitful and multiply, and fill the earth and subdue it; and have dominion over the fish of the sea and over the birds of the air and over every living thing that moves on the earth" (Gen. 1:28). Every Christian church echoes this sentiment in challenging us to treat mother earth with care. Although "dominion" is not an altogether inappropriate term for being environmentally responsible, some suggest that dominion may be misunderstood as wanton power, the freedom to abuse the earth and our atmosphere at will. As stewards of God's good creation, we are obliged to take care of this fragile cosmos in the way its divine Creator would want.

Recent literature in environmental ethics suggests two conceptual shifts. First, let's conceive of the cosmos as a living reality, an ecosystem to which we belong, rather than a material world placed at our disposal. James Gustafson calls this a more cosmos-centered view of creation as distinct from an anthropocentric view, which sees ourselves as the reason all else exists, not unlike a spoiled child's self-centeredness. Second, by contrast, we are called to live more "in harmony with" nature, rather than in "dominion over" it. In one sense it is merely a matter of semantics. But in a larger sense, by seeing ourselves as one with creation, part of a greater cosmic plan, we more humbly engage our ecosystem and better realize the fragile interconnected balance of it all.

Q. 77. So are we morally obliged to recycle cans, newspapers, plastic, and other household waste materials?

Yes, but such domestic conservation is only a first step; there are also the more massive issues of clean air and water, toxic and nuclear wastes, diminishing natural resources, the depleted ozone layer, the ravaging of the rain forests, melting polar icecaps, endangered species, and world population. As with economic questions, so too with our environmental issues, we must ask what our present policies—individual, corporate, and governmental—do *for the environment*, positively speaking, as well as what these policies do *to the environment*, negatively speaking.

Environmental sins are social sins, systemic evils, which require not only personal vigilance, but corporate and governmental commitment as well. It is not cheap to prevent environmental damage in the first place or to clean up past mistakes or excesses. Profit margins will be encroached upon and tax relief will be forestalled if we take seriously our responsibility to live "in harmony with" God's creation—an awesome, energy-rich, interconnected, cosmically fragile universe. Recycling, conservation, and other "eco-sensitive" lifestyle changes bespeak a growing consciousness and greater sense of personal responsibility about our environment. We are continually invited and challenged to be God's partners, cocreators in the ongoing project of refashioning the world anew, "boldly going where no one has gone before."

Q. 78. What is the relationship between civil law and morality?

The beginnings of an answer to this question can be found in question 62 above. There we noted that law is a narrower, more restricted concept than morality. Morality is about what is objectively right or wrong, what contributes to or detracts from personal and communal well-being. Morality and God's will or God's law are one and the same; however, we don't try to legislate into civil law everything that we think is good and right. Nor do we try to outlaw, by statute, everything that we believe is harmful or sinful. The goal of society as a whole is morality itself, the common good or well-being of each and all, whereas the goal of government and its laws is a bit narrower, namely, public order—fostering an environment of basic justice and relative peace, in which people have the freedom and mobility to make their own life choices. As the Evangelical Lutheran Church Assembly defines it, "the state [i.e., government] is responsible under God for the protection of its citizens and the maintenance of justice *and public order*" (Orlando, 1991).

Society enacts three kinds of laws: (1) criminal codes to punish serious abuses of basic human rights, needs, and dignity; (2) laws designed to educate people to choose wisely (e.g., mandatory food and drug labeling); and (3) laws offering incentives to promote positive behavior or to improve public safety and health (e.g., tax rebates and government grants).

My main concern here is to dispel the notion that if something isn't illegal it is thereby morally right. Not so. For example, at one time a number of consensual sexual practices were prohibited by many local or state criminal laws (e.g., sodomy, oral sex, adultery, fornication). At some point, because of changing societal mores and concerns about the tactics used to enforce such laws (e.g., bedroom surveillance, bugging devices, etc.), these sexual practices were removed from the criminal code in most states and municipalities. That does not mean that the morality or immorality of each action changed with the stroke of a governor's or mayor's pen, but such actions were thought to be better resolved in the personal moral sphere than in the realm of law.

In the same way, capital punishment was legal in the United States prior to 1967. From 1967 to 1976 the Supreme Court imposed a legal moratorium on capital punishment, primarily because of concerns that it was being inequitably imposed in certain regions of the country. Since 1976 capital punishment once again has been legally allowed, but on a state-by-state basis. This does not mean that the execution of prisoners for capital crimes was moral prior to 1967, became immoral for a nine-year period between 1967 and 1976, and once again became moral thereafter in certain states. The morality of capital punishment continues to be hotly debated (see QQ. 88–91). During this ongoing period of societal debate about the morality of capital punishment, what should the law be? Should we be more restrictive, not allowing any executions, in case we eventually discern that capital punishment is immoral? Or should we follow the old maxim "Where there is doubt, there is freedom to choose and act"? Law and morality are related, but not identical.

Two brief conclusions seem apropos. First, beware of simplistically linking law and morality when contemplating whom to vote for in elections. Some groups assume that if you agree with them about a moral issue, you will automatically adopt their approach to civil legislation. People of good will may agree about a controversial moral issue, such as abortion, and still disagree as to what sort of law is best for fostering public order around that topic. It is wrong to assume that one who disagrees with your legal opinion is automatically on the opposite side of the moral question involved. There is and rightly ought to be room for intramural legal debates among people who share identical moral conclusions.

Second, one can be a loyal citizen of one's city, state, or nation without completely agreeing with that community's laws or public officials. The concept of "loyal opposition" bespeaks well the right of a citizen to advocate legislative change or the ouster of a given elected or appointed civil official. The old adages "America, love it or leave it" and "My country, right or wrong" are not morally sound principles. One can certainly love one's community and at the same time disagree with some of its legal statutes. Morality is a fuller, more inclusive reality. The tradition of "conscientious objection" reflects this notion of a civil community's respect for the integrity of conscience of those loyal citizens who disagree with a certain legal policy. In a truly just and humane society there even ought to be room for nonviolent protest and civil disobedience (see Q. 87).

Q. **79. Haven't we wandered pretty far from the Ten Commandments in these questions about political and economic morality?**

I don't think so. I think we have cast the discussion in a broader, more positive context—human dignity, common good, rights, and justice—but it is still about fundamental "thou shalts" and "thou shalt nots." When discussing the morality of politics, the economy, and business we are basically unpacking three of the Ten Commandments: "You shall not steal. . . . You shall not bear false witness against your neighbor. . . . You shall not covet your neighbor's house . . . or anything that belongs to your neighbor" (Exod. 20:15–17; Deut. 5:19–21). To focus solely on the negative prohibitions would rob our Christian morality of its life-giving force. Going beyond the Ten Commandments, we are called to walk the extra mile, turn the other cheek, and give in excess of the strict limits of justice. These are the earmarks of true Christians.

So in this series of questions on political and economic life, I have tried to explain our twenty centuries of church tradition with a degree of sophistication and nuance, realizing that social questions beg easy answers. One of my mentors is fond of saying, "It's all very complex." He suggests that this statement should be our opening comment whenever we deal with a social ethics question in the political or economic sphere. That response is not meant to forestall honest answers, but rather to acknowledge that discerning justice and fostering a degree of mercy in public and corporate dealings require a surgeon's scalpel more than a crusader's broadsword. Discerning truth from falsehood, fact from fabrication, honesty from self-serving chatter, all within a framework of multifaceted justice—this truly requires the wisdom of Solomon, the patience of Job, the two-edged sword of Paul, and the mercy of Christ Jesus.

Q. **80. Is there any political or economic commandment that is uniquely or distinctively Christian?**

It is important to note that moral rightness and wrongness are objective or universal, not cornered by any specific religion or denomination. Moral truth transcends church membership or doctrine. For example, lying, cheating, and stealing are morally wrong not only for Christians and not exclusively because we are Christian. The concept of a *natural law* or *objective morality*, which we discussed in the opening section of this book (QQ. 3–4, 12–14), suggests that there is a law written in every human heart, an infused sense of right and wrong, which can be discovered by all persons of good will who conscientiously seek truth and goodness (see Rom. 2:15). So, in the broadest sense, there is no command to do right that obliges Christians but exempts others who sincerely seek God, truth, and goodness.

However, given the distinctiveness of the Christian story, the message of the dying and rising made possible through, with, and in Jesus Christ, we Christians may have certain emphases, priorities, and graced insights into moral living. One of these is as old as our Hebrew Scripture roots and as fresh as today. Following the example of Jesus, Christians profess a special degree or kind of concern for the voiceless, "the lost, the least, and the last" in our midst. God in Christ has so loved, forgiven, and redeemed us that we should similarly incarnate this kind of magnanimous, no-strings-attached, unconditional love for others, particularly those most in need.

In recent years some have called this a "preferential option for the poor." By "poor" is meant not only those in financial need, but anyone whose basic dignity is on the line. The Hebrew law and prophets again and again called the chosen people to defend the oppressed and the outcast—"the widow, the orphan, and the stranger" (Deut. 10:18; 14:29; Isa. 1:17; 51:14; 61:1-2). When Jesus stood up in his hometown synagogue he echoed Isaiah's prophecy by proclaiming: "The Spirit of the Lord is upon me, because he has anointed me to bring good news to the poor. He has sent me to proclaim release to the captives and recovery of sight to the blind, to let the oppressed go free, to proclaim the year of the Lord's favor" (Luke 4:18). And finally, Jesus said that at the last judgment we will be asked to give an accounting of our corporal works of mercy to those in need—the hungry, thirsty, poorly clothed, homeless, sick, and imprisoned (Matt. 25:31-46).

If there is or ought to be one earmark of Christians and their church communities it should be that we champion the rights and needs of those most marginalized in our wider society. We are called to act as lobbyists for the voiceless. We champion the cause of the *anawim*, God's little ones, those most in need and least able to fend for or defend themselves. For when we serve the needs of "these least ones," we are doing it to and for Christ himself. In this area we all could learn a lesson from Christian witnesses like Francis and Clare, Vincent de Paul, Albert Schweitzer, Dorothy Day, Martin Luther King, Jr., and Mother Teresa. May we, as individuals and as communities of faith, better practice what we preach.

Issues in Peacemaking, Capital Punishment, and Violence

Q. 81. If Jesus Christ is the Prince of Peace, how can his followers in every age so easily justify war, breaking the commandment "Thou shalt not kill"?

That is a good question and one that requires a complex answer, not rationalization or double-speak. There seems little doubt that Jesus, especially as described in Matthew's Gospel, calls us to be peacemakers, not warriors. His Sermon on the Mount opens with the beatitudes, including "Blessed are the peacemakers, for they will be called children of God" (5:9). Within the same chapter Jesus admonishes his followers, "You have heard that it was said, 'An eye for an eye and a tooth for a tooth.' But I say to you, Do not resist an evildoer. But if anyone strikes you on the right cheek, turn the other also" (5:38–39). All of this is within the framework of the command "Love your enemies and pray for those who persecute you" (5:43).

Jesus' own actions matched his words. He rebuked Peter for raising a sword against those who came to arrest him (John 18:10–11). When he stood before Pilate, who noted that he had been handed over by his own people, Jesus replied, "My kingdom is not from this world. If my kingdom were from this world, my followers would be fighting to keep me from being handed over" (John 18:36). So he was led off to be crucified, though no person was ever more innocent when led to the slaughter. Jesus and his first-century followers seem to have been absolute pacifists, unwilling to take up the weapons of war. They were willing to face persecution and injustice rather than bear arms, even against unjust aggressors.

How did this community of peacemakers evolve into the church that devised the so-called just-war tradition? And is this a faithful evolution of Christian morality or an aberration and a cop-out? Certainly those who belong to the peace churches—the Quakers, the Amish, and the Mennonites—see as timeless Jesus' call to be pacifists, countercultural, and sectlike. Like a city on a hill or a lamp on a lampstand, Christians should openly oppose evil with good, hatred with love, and violence with peaceful acceptance or, at most, nonviolent protest. Across the centuries those Christians who lived as absolute pacifists (e.g., Francis of Assisi) have served as symbols, beacons of hope and challenge, prophets crying in the wilderness of a world that too often flirts with evil by dabbling or even immersing itself in war.

The early Christians were pacifists at least in part because they thought the second coming of Jesus, the end of the world, would be soon—within a matter of months or years but surely within their lifetime. Why worry about redressing earthly grievances if this world of political communities would soon give way to the fullness of Christ's reign? Paul's two letters to the Thessalonians were written to deal with the concerns that arose as time passed and people died but Jesus still hadn't returned in glory. If the end is *not* near, then are we Christians more obliged to engage in the politics and military affairs of our present world, striving either to make it a safer and better community, or at least not to allow it to degenerate further into chaos?

As the first century A.D. faded into the second and third, the Roman army became more of a police force, protecting the now-established empire, rather than serving as an army of conquest. In 312, with the conversion of Emperor Constantine to Christianity, all required military oaths to the pagan gods ceased, removing at least one obstacle to Christians' participating in military service. It was at this point that theologians and bishops like St. Ambrose and later St. Augustine began to ask whether there is any moral justification for a society having a military and whether Christians might rightly be able to serve as soldiers. Scripturally they highlighted Jesus' encounter with the centurion, whose appreciation of military command and obedience Jesus did not condemn but rather held up as admirable (Matt. 8:5–13; Luke 7:2–10). Or one finds in the Gospel of Luke, "Soldiers also asked him [John the Baptist], 'And we, what should we do?' He said to them, 'Do not extort money from anyone by threats or false accusation, and be satisfied with your wages'"

(Luke 3:14). Neither Jesus nor John the Baptist seems to condemn soldiers as such, nor do they challenge them to lay down their arms and become pacifists. While this is in no way a resounding gospel approval of war, it does lend some credence to the later writings of Ambrose, Augustine, and Thomas Aquinas, who defended the use of military force in certain restricted situations.

Q. **82. What exactly are those situations in which war or military action is justified?**

Most scripture scholars and a number of scripture translations today suggest that the commandment "Thou shalt not kill" was never a simple prohibition against all killing. Rather, it might better be translated, as the New Revised Standard Version suggests, as "You shall not murder" (Deut. 5:17; Exod. 20:13). Across the centuries Christians have nuanced and refined this commandment by saying that one ought never to kill *the innocent* or one ought never to kill *without justification*. Thus, killing in self-defense, which some argue is not intentional killing at all, has traditionally been exempt from the biblical prohibition. In addition, killing within a justified war or killing to protect the community from an unjust aggressor (i.e., capital punishment) have been defended as the exceptions that prove the otherwise exceptionless commandment against directly taking human life.

It has been argued that while you or I, as individuals, might live up to the Christian ideal of complete nonviolence as absolute pacifists, the state and its chosen leaders are entrusted with the duty to protect the innocent and weaker members of the community against aggression from within or without. It follows from this duty, that the ruler or government has an obligation to police within the nation's borders and to defend by military means beyond their nation's borders against unjustified assault or attack.

As Augustine (354–430) and Thomas Aquinas (1225–1274) conceived of it, one must fulfill a certain set of conditions before one can even contemplate entering into a war, in which soldiers knowingly kill human beings in an opposing military force. These conditions are known as *jus ad bellum* (i.e., justification toward a war). So also, once the war has begun, contrary to the old cliche "All is fair in love and war," all levels and means of destruction are not automatically justified. The rules for fairness and limitation within war are known as *jus in bello* (i.e., justification in war). Laying down one's own life or taking the life of someone else may be justified, regrettably, for the sake of protecting the innocent or restoring core values and conditions essential to humane survival and community.

Since the fourth century, mainline Christians have accepted that war itself may be justified if these *jus ad bellum* principles are met: (1) just cause; (2) declared by competent authority; (3) conducted with a proper intention; (4) last resort; (5) probability of success; (6) proportionality; and (7) comparative justice.

What constitutes *just cause* for war? Self-defense against unjust aggression would be the overarching reason. Under that, one might list protection of the innocent (children, elderly, infirm, noncombatants) and the defense or reassertion of basic human rights— a climate in which liberty, justice, truth, and love once again may flourish. Given especially the massive destructive potential of modern weapons of war, the cause must be clear and of sufficient gravity to risk such harm.

Why must war be *declared by competent or proper authority*? This serves two purposes. First, war is not justified if it breaks out as a brawl or a factional dispute among feuding clans or gangs or mobs. It can only be called a justified war if a duly elected or appointed head of state follows legal procedures to commit the community to this last resort, this lethal course of action. Second, the proper authority in charge is capable of surrendering, signing the peace, or calling an armistice. War is so destructive, that we must have a rightful means to enter it and to exit, which "declaration by proper authority" attempts to guarantee.

What is meant by a *proper intention*? If one's sole or primary motive is revenge, or economic profit and plunder, or a desire for genocide and "ethnic cleansing," or some other base motive, then even if one has just cause to declare war, one is morally tainted by these ignoble intentions. Right intention means that one's exclusive aim is to redress the grievance of the just cause, to defend the innocent, and to secure the peace as soon as possible. All lesser motives, while natural and emotionally understandable, ought not to be our chosen intentions.

Obviously, one ought not to take up arms unless all other avenues for diplomatic and negotiated settlement have been exhausted. War, if undertaken, must really be the *last resort,* a regrettable final option in the repertoire of a true peacemaker. Moreover, if one foresees little or no likelihood of *success,* then declaring war is suicidal and foolish. One is reminded of Jesus' story about the king going out to wage war, who first calculated his own troop strength as compared to that of his opponent, to determine whether doing battle or suing for peace might be the wiser course (Luke 14:31–33).

Proportionality and *comparative justice* dovetail into the question of means and end. Is our cause vital enough, essential enough, good enough, when weighed against the potential loss of human life and property on both sides? If we win, but with few civilians left alive, with the earth scorched and unable to yield new life, then the cost is "out of proportion." Our just cause would not be sufficient or "comparable" to the harm foreseen.

If, and only if, all seven conditions are met, might a Christian individual or society be willing to enter on the road to war. The late Paul Ramsey, an articulate Methodist ethicist, suggested that the term "just war" is too benign for the horrible reality that war is. He used the term "justified war" to remind us that while it may, as a last resort, sometimes be necessary (i.e., justified), we ought never to conceive of war as good or desirable, in that sense, just. Christians must always strive to be peacemakers. If war should become justified or necessary, Christians ought to enter it reluctantly, for it is surely, at best, only the lesser of two evils, *not* a noble crusade.

Q. 83. You mentioned that even within war there are limits to what we morally can do. What are those *jus in bello* principles?

The two *jus in bello* principles are *proportionality* and *discrimination* (also known as the principle of noncombatant immunity). As each military battle, operation, or campaign is planned one must ask, Is this worth it? Will the objective to be gained justify the amount of force and the destruction foreseen? For example, is taking possession of a given village or island or mountaintop of enough strategic importance to offset the estimated loss of life and property? If so, forge ahead. If not, such an operation is not morally defensible.

With the introduction of nuclear weaponry many times more powerful than the bombs dropped on Hiroshima and Nagasaki, all nuclear nations have been forced to ask whether such weapons are categorically out of proportion to strategic battlefield targets and intrawar goals.

Second, across the Christian centuries, there has been a fairly consistent prohibition of war tactics aimed against civilian or noncombatant populations. Schools, residential neighborhoods, medical facilities, and other civilian population centers ought never to be the focus of military bombing or attack. Likewise, even military hospitals, base chapels, and similar service centers ought to be off-limits as military targets. That does not mean that munitions factories or supply lines or similar military-oriented facilities may not be considered reasonable targets. Thus, some civilians, whether those directly involved in such depots and factories or those who reside nearby, may be killed in such bombings or raids. However, according to the just-war theory, this so-called collateral damage may be tolerated, if it is truly an *indirect* and *unintentional* loss, provided our focus is clearly and solely on the military objective.

Q. 84. I have heard it said that the just-war theory doesn't apply in the nuclear age. Do you agree?

I think what some people mean by that statement is that given the massive numbers and power of modern nuclear weapons, perhaps no war, at least not on a global scale, would ever be justifiable. The potential destruction, including the possible annihilation of the entire planet, would seem to be categorically out of proportion to any boundary-related or rights dispute. However, it seems to me that this judgment does not supersede the just-war tradition, but is actually an illustration of the just-war theory at work. It is precisely by applying the principle of proportionality and by questioning whether noncombatant immunity can ever be guaranteed when nuclear weapons are unleashed that one may come to the conclusion that nuclear war can't be justified. Thus, rather than making the just-war principles obsolete, their application to this new military technology seems to demonstrate that they are still a valid ethical tool, flexible, adaptable, and still of vital importance in evaluating war now, as in the past.

In 1983 the Catholic bishops of the United States applied these principles to the state of global and American policy. Their document, *The Challenge of Peace: God's Promise and Our Response*, serves as an excellent primer for Christian peacemakers, for those who advocate absolute pacificism as well as for those who are willing to tread gently on the slippery slope of the principles of a "justified" war. In a similar vein, the United Methodist Council of Bishops issued *In Defense of Creation: The Nuclear Crisis and a Just Peace* in 1986, as their contribution to this society-wide debate. Paul Ramsey's hand can be seen in this carefully refined approach to justifying war only as a last and regrettable resort. These documents, as well as others drafted by various mainline Christian churches, attempt to bring the complex and nuanced Christian just-war tradition to bear on the questions of peace and war in our own time and place.

Q. **85. I know it's a thorny issue, but how do you evaluate morally the dropping of the atomic bombs on Hiroshima and Nagasaki in 1945?**

Responding to this question is sure to cause controversy among various readers of this volume. After you read what I have to say, I invite you to reflect on it prayerfully and to discuss it civilly with one another. There is a tendency not to want to admit that one's own nation has ever made a mistake. There is also a tendency, despite the just-war criteria, to say that anything goes in war. "If they started it, we'll finish it, whatever it takes!" Finally, there is a tendency to say that the end justifies the means if it saves more of our soldiers' lives.

When all is said and done, with due respect to President Truman's subjective sincerity, I do not see how we can apply the just-war criteria honestly and endorse the dropping of atomic bombs on two clearly civilian population centers. As with the Nazi saturation bombing of London by conventional weapons and the Allied counterbombing of Dresden and Berlin near the end of World War II, such massive destruction that was focused on noncombatant population centers seems to me to be prohibited by the principles of discrimination and due proportion.

Those who defend these saturation bombings or the atomic drops on Japan do so by a raw consequentialism—the end (quicker conclusion of the war) justifies the means (annihilating civilians so as to demoralize the enemy, causing them to surrender sooner). In the case of Hiroshima and Nagasaki the decision was arrived at by projecting the potential duration of the war and estimating the number of lives that might be lost. While some may debate the accuracy of the projections, those who defend Truman's decision do so by valuing American military lives more than Japanese military *or civilian* lives. It is that inclusion of civilians as expendable, rather than untouchable, that seems clearly to breach the just-war tradition.

There is no way of knowing how long the war would have lasted if the atomic bombs had not been dropped in August 1945. Scholars stack their data on both sides of this debate, some claiming that Japan would have surrendered soon no matter what, others claiming that they would have fought on to the last soldier or military unit. Critics of the American decision suggest that we could have bombed some deserted Japanese island as a warning, and that if such a warning failed to bring Japanese surrender an atomic bomb could have been dropped on a major *military* target. The events of Hiroshima and Nagasaki, now a half century old, stand as a reminder that the just-war tradition must be applied with great caution and integrity. And may those absolute pacifists among us always stand as a beacon of idealism, challenging us to be "just peacemakers," not "just warriors."

Q. 86. What about revolutions and civil war? How do they fit into the scheme of things, morally speaking?

That's an interesting question, especially since the faction that revolts or secedes has no "proper authority" to declare war and, in some sense, is showing disrespect to the duly constituted head of state, who, according to tradition, somehow shares in God's own authority. Various Christian documents of this century defend the right of citizens to rise up against tyrannical or unjust leaders. Hitler, Mussolini, Stalin, Idi Amin, and the former government of South Africa all come to mind as potential examples of "unjust aggressors" holding legal power. True peace is not merely the absence of war. Oppression, injustice, gestapo-like repression, intolerable living conditions, and the denial of basic human freedoms all constitute a species of violence, whether direct or indirect. The fact that some charismatic leaders tend to rise to prominence in righteous opposition movements (e.g., Nelson Mandela, Yasir Arafat, Gerry Adams) indicates that we might be able to extend the "proper authority" provision of the just-war tradition to include these acknowledged leaders of opposition parties or movements, provided their cause is just and the potential outbreak of armed hostilities is truly the threatened last resort.

Fortunately for the people of South Africa, the injustice of apartheid finally was redressed by relatively peaceful means, instead of all-out civil war. Whether the Israelis and Palestinians can bring their first plantings for peace to full bloom is still unclear. The Nobel Peace Prize given to the leaders of these opposing nations may have been a bit premature, but it was intended to foster diplomacy over the continued threat of war and the interim outbursts of violence and terrorism. The fragile armistice between the two sides in Northern Ireland also holds some promise that a long-standing warlike situation may not erupt into full-scale revolution, provided some compromise and negotiation can bring about a reasonably just settlement. Yes, with some adaptations, the just-war principles could and do apply to domestic instances of injustice and potential revolution.

Q. 87. What does the Christian tradition have to say about the morality of conscientious objection?

In their pastoral constitution on the church in the world, the Catholic leaders at Vatican II declared:

> In this same spirit we cannot help but express our admiration for all who forgo the use of violence to vindicate their rights and resort to other means of defense which are available to weaker parties, provided it can be done without harm to the rights and duties of others in the community. (*Church in the Modern World,* #78)

This was a major step for the Roman Catholic community. While other peace churches have long supported the right of someone in good conscience to be an absolute pacifist or conscientious objector, the Catholic church and some of the mainline Protestant churches have, until recently, had little room for such avowed non-combatants, especially during the two world wars of this century. Particularly in light of the fact that Hitler's aggression made World War II almost a textbook case for the *jus ad bellum* principles, there was little sympathy for those who opposed that war, even if they were opposed to *all* war.

It would seem that the laws of a civilized nation ought to make provision for those potential draftees who, in good conscience, believe that they could never take up arms and kill another human being, no matter how just the cause or how properly the war is declared. Their decision, made in good conscience, is inviolable; that is, it ought not to be violated—by them or by us. (See Q. 13.) This does not mean that they are exempt from serving their nation in time of distress. They may accept an appointment to do alternative noncombatant service in the military (medic, chaplain's assistant, cook, clerk). However, some conscientious objectors believe that such support services contribute to the overall military effort, making them accomplices in the killing done on the battlefield. These pacifists may accept alternative service at home, whether on a highway construction crew, in the national parks, or in some other government-related service. If, however, a conscientious objector believes that by doing this task on the homefront he frees someone to take up arms on the battlefield, he may refuse this alternative service as well. Finally, if one cannot in good conscience perform any parallel noncombatant service, then one may face imprisonment either for the duration of the war or for some specified amount of time.

In any of these scenarios, society is striving to respect the individual's sincerity and integrity of conscience while at the same time demanding that he or she not shirk one's duty to serve the community in some capacity. The sincerity of those who conscientiously serve in the military as well as that of those who in good conscience refuse to serve both deserve our respect. Name-calling or assuming ulterior motives on either side is uncalled for, un-Christian, and disrespectful of the integrity of each person's conscience regarding a moral issue of profound importance to persons of good will on both sides.

There is also the case of a person who is a *selective* conscientious objector, that is, someone who is not opposed in theory to all war but who believes that a given war is unjustified or that a given command within war is contrary to the *jus in bello* principles for just conduct. Obviously, it would be difficult for an army to take a vote on each military action, allowing those who dissent to "sit this one out." Therefore, if one accepts a commission into the military one is expected, all things being equal, to obey orders and to meet military objectives. If, however, one is asked to enter into a conflict that one truly believes is unjustified or to perform an action that one deeply believes to be disproportionate or indiscriminate, then he or she is obliged to follow that conscience decision and to refuse. There will be a price for such refusal, but one has to be true to oneself, even at the risk of ridicule, hazing, or military proceedings.

It is incumbent on good civilian and military leaders to discern *jus ad bellum* and *jus in bello* principles carefully, in order to garner the unflagging loyalty of their troops and to forestall any such qualms of conscience in combat. The just-war tradition is a helpful tool; but it is not a mathematical formula, and, in real-life situations, it can lend itself to rationalization. Prudence, a sense of justice, and courage are some of the virtues required of a discerning Christian and humane peacemaker.

It should be noted that the role of conscientious objector is not limited to military questions. Whenever a society has seriously erred and seems unwilling to reexamine or change unjust, bigoted, or immoral practices (i.e., social sin), then faithful citizens are obliged to stand up. If they can influence the system by civil discourse and electoral change, then that is the preferred course. If, however, the cause is serious enough, then it is morally justified for citizens to resort to civil disobedience, nonviolent protest, and other acts of conscientious objection. Their goal is both to be true to their own consciences and to impact and change society's intransigence.

Q. **88. Shifting focus to another issue of societally condoned killing, what does Christianity have to say about the death penalty?**

In Jesus' lifetime the death penalty, or capital punishment, was an accepted fact of life. The right of the state to protect the common good of all by executing those criminals deemed dangerous and irreformable was an integral part of the judicial and penal system of the Roman Empire. However, as Jesus' own case indicates, sometimes mistakes are made and an innocent person is put to death. There is no recourse, no due process, no way to correct the mistake or repair the damage once a person has been falsely executed.

Still, across the Christian centuries people have looked to selected passages in the Old and New Testaments to defend use of the death penalty. In the book of Genesis we find the story of God addressing Noah, "Whoever sheds the blood of a human, by a human shall that person's blood be shed" (Gen. 9:6). Even more vividly there is a whole section of Exodus devoted to capital crimes and punishment: "Whoever strikes a person mortally shall be put to death. . . . But if someone willfully attacks and kills another by treachery, you shall take the killer from my altar for execution" (Exod. 21:12–14). And nine verses later one finds the famous passage: "If any harm follows, then you shall give life for life, eye for eye, tooth for tooth, hand for hand, foot for foot, burn for burn, wound for wound, stripe for stripe" (Exod. 21:23–25).

In the New Testament, the Letter to the Romans defends the divine right of governments to act in God's name: "But if you do what is wrong, you should be afraid, for the authority does not bear the sword in vain! It is the servant of God to execute wrath on the wrongdoer" (Rom. 13:4). Despite Jesus' command to love our enemies, to forgive those who do us wrong, and his direct negation of "an eye for an eye" (Matt. 5:38–48; 6:14–15; 18:21–35), the call for vengeance against criminals and just retribution can be heard in most Christian communities as it can be within the wider society.

While individual citizens may not take it upon themselves to execute evildoers, the state has that right, in the name of divine authority and as an exercise of its duty to protect the common good. The arguments in favor of capital punishment are grounded, as is the just-war tradition, in the right and duty of the state to protect its citizens from unjust aggression. If this can be done by prison sentences or other punitive means short of execution, so much the better. However, if the life of a guilty capital criminal must be sacrificed to guarantee the safety of the innocent majority, then so be it. As Thomas Aquinas summed it up:

> [I]t is lawful to kill an evildoer in so far as it is directed to the welfare of the whole community, so that it belongs to him alone who has charge of the community's welfare. . . . Now the care of the common

good is entrusted to persons of rank having public authority: where-
fore they alone, and not private individuals, can lawfully put evildoers to death. (*Summa Theologica* II,II 64.3)

In addition, Aquinas reflected a common emotional response
expressed by victims of serious crime when he suggested: "Hence,
although it be evil in itself to kill a man so long as he preserve his
dignity, yet it may be good to kill a man who has sinned, even as it is
to kill a beast. For a bad man is worse than a beast, and is more
harmful, as the Philosopher [Aristotle] states" (*Summa Theologica*
II,II 64.2). His former argument, that the state has the right and
obligation to protect its citizens, even by wielding the sword when
necessary, remains compelling for many Christian churches and
their official theologies. However, it seems contrary to our core
Christian belief in *the inherent and abiding dignity of every human life*
to declare that even the most wretched, misguided, or mentally
deranged criminals are no longer human and thus deserve to be
treated as "beasts." Such criminal members of our communities are
to be feared and guarded against for sure, but also to be pitied for
their warped minds and/or mental illness.

Q. 89. If capital punishment has been accepted as moral by
the mainline churches across the centuries, why do so
many Christian denominations seem to be opposed to it
today?

Defense of the death penalty throughout history has been built on
the assumptions that only the guilty will be executed and that their
extermination is the only way to protect the rest of us against their
crimes. In the last two decades a number of major Christian denominations—American Baptists, Disciples of Christ, Episcopalians,
Lutherans, Roman Catholics, Presbyterians—have gone on record
expressing their misgivings about the fairness and effectiveness of
capital punishment. Traditionally, punishment has been seen as
having three beneficial effects: (1) *retribution* or *revenge* for past misdeeds (paying one's due back to the community); (2) *deterrence* of
future crimes (both by this criminal and by others); (3) *reform* or
rehabilitation of the criminal himself/herself.

With the exception of a deathbed conversion, it would seem that the third effect is negated by the death penalty. The prisoner is no longer alive to repent, reform, or be rehabilitated. So the major moral questions revolve around how effective capital punishment is as a deterrent and whether the desire for vengeance or retribution is sufficient to override our strong Christian mandate against killing people. Obviously, execution permanently prevents this particular criminal from future acts of violence. He or she is dead. The personal crime spree is over. However, there is little statistical or hard evidence to indicate that the periodic execution of a criminal deters other murderers, rapists, thieves, or spies from plying their immoral professions.

In theory, one might assume that the threat of losing one's life—if caught, convicted, and sentenced—would deter potential criminals from risking their lives for ill-gotten gain. In reality, most murders either are crimes of passion within families and among friends, for which there is little or no premeditation, or are carefully planned and executed by well-paid assassins or "hit men," who seem to thrive on the danger and risk more than fear it. Some studies indicate that a third variety of killer is so depressed and plagued by low self-esteem that he or she secretly courts death, practically wishing to be killed in the act or to be caught and executed. In all three instances, the threat of capital punishment would seem to have little or no deterrent effect.

In addition, given the sad state of our criminal justice system, one's chances for being caught, successfully tried, sentenced to death, and ultimately executed after a series of almost mandatory appeals are small. This leads many scholars and Christian groups to conclude that the deterrent effect is mythical more than actual. To counter this concern, some recommend more aggressive police investigations, swifter court trials, and a minimum of due process in terms of appeal. The former two—more police and courts—would be financially costly, and the latter—reducing one's right to appeal—arguably would threaten the constitutional rights of the innocent. Are we willing to spend the necessary public monies to improve our criminal justice system? Is the answer to the yearly increase in capital crime to hire more police and build bigger jails? Are there not root causes of crime that could better be attacked with our energy and money? Does a denial of the various levels of the appeal process increase the likelihood that an innocent person will be executed by a miscarriage of justice? Some Christian denominations worry that such proposals to enhance the hazy deterrent effect of the death penalty may be at a cost that is too high, both financially and in terms of human rights.

Q. **90. But doesn't the family of a victim have the right to see their loved one's murderer punished?**

You are speaking now not about deterring future crime but about the gut-level, visceral desire to have capital criminals pay the ultimate price—in the gas chamber, in the electric chair, by hanging, or by lethal injection. Is this desire for retribution, more commonly called vengeance or revenge, sufficient for Christians to forgo our primary call for mercy, compassion, forgiveness, and an abiding sense of respect for the dignity of all persons, even those least deserving of our respect? The leaders of many Christian churches today are saying that the price is too high, that fostering vengeance demeans us more than humanizes us. Yes, there is an emotional, almost animal desire to wreak vengeance, to make the criminal suffer. And yes, capital criminals should pay a high price for their crimes, both as a matter of justice and in order to safeguard the rest of us. Life in prison, with no option for parole, would seem to satisfy both concerns—a major penalty for the perpetrator and security for all from his/her future acts.

What about the financial costs of execution versus lifelong imprisonment? According to a recent study, the highest *annual cost per prisoner* in a state penal institution is in Alaska ($28,215); the lowest is in Arkansas ($7,557); and the national average in state prisons is $15,586 and in federal penitentiaries is $14,456 (*U.S.A. Today*, 17 March 1995, using 1993 data). Projecting this cost over a twenty-to-thirty-year life span and measuring it against the projected costs of multiple judicial appeals of a conviction (attorney and court costs as well as incarceration during the process) offer little evidence to suggest that either alternative is noticeably cheaper or terribly cost-effective. The financial debate about lifetime imprisonment versus execution seems to be a stalemate at best.

Yet, while the clergy and leadership of many Christian denominations support the abolition of the death penalty, that position is opposed by many lay Christians in the pews. People are enraged about the rise in violent crimes and a fear that if we don't stem the tide, things will only get worse. Between 1983 and 1990 the number of violent crimes in the United States increased from 1.25 million per year to just over 1.8 million. That means 550,000 *additional* crimes of violence in a given year. Murder is up from 19,310 deaths in 1983 to 23,440 deaths in 1990, a loss of 4,130 *additional* lives (F.B.I. Crime Report for 1990). Many citizens feel overwhelmed and, like the exasperated character in the film *Network*, want to scream out, "I'm not gonna take it anymore!" Too often they latch onto the supposed quick fix: "Let's execute them all and build bigger prisons for the rest." Rage and fear and a sense of helplessness in the face of rising crime are real.

In their 1994 message *Community Violence*, the Evangelical Lutheran Church Council asserts:

> "Tough on crime" policy stances are often proposed in response to the fear of violent crimes. Such stances have their place, but also their limits. Although police and prisons help to protect society, they have no real effect on the *causes* of violence. . . . Instead of addressing the root causes of violence, "tough on crime" measures can blind us to the injustices that breed violence in the first place.

I think that the Christian leaders who recognize deeper causes of violence and offer more long-range solutions have done their homework better than many well-meaning people who vent their raw fears and frustrations. Capital punishment can surely be defended, in theory, with various arguments from the scriptures and Christian tradition. But when we come to real life in the 1990s, in practice, many churches believe that capital punishment has outlived its usefulness. Because it fails to deter, because it fosters a mind-set of vengeance, and because it preempts us from seeking fuller, long-term solutions, perhaps we ought to say it is time to retire the death penalty, not to reinstitute it. This is surely countercultural. It is surely not the popular opinion. But I think it is truly an example of prophetically bringing the light of the gospel to bear on contemporary problems.

Q. **91. As long as we give criminals fair trials and reasonable due process to appeal, why shouldn't we rejoice when justice finally is done?**

Provided the person is truly guilty as charged, there seems to be a fine line between appreciating that justice has been served and what some mean by "rejoicing." If one feels some sense of relief, regret that it had to come to this, and some kind of closure to a horrible chain of events, then perhaps one can be said to be responding reasonably and appropriately, though other people feel little contentment at the thought of another's execution. However, it is not uncommon for some citizens, particularly relatives or friends of the criminal's victims, to request tickets to witness an execution. Others gather in groups outside prisons, set up barbeque grills, share coolers full of beer, sell souvenirs, and generally have a festive party. Some of the T-shirts and poster slogans at one such tailgate party included: "Roast in Peace," "Burn Bundy Burn," "Tuesday is Fryday," "Buckle Up," and "Scramble Him." If this is what is meant by "rejoicing," I think it is warped and bears no resemblance to righteousness or justice. My fear is that too many Christians hover closer to this latter response than to a rightful, but regretful sense of relief or finality. Each of us must take our own moral pulse to ask whether we respond humanely and appropriately to the public killing of certain tragically evil or misguided fellow human beings.

A second concern is voiced by those who follow sociological data concerning those executed over the past half century. There seems to have been and still to be a disproportionate number of males, people of color, and persons of lower socioeconomic level on death row, and far more in southern states than in the north. The simple answer might be that more capital crimes are committed by poor black or hispanic males than by people who are better off economically, white, or female. There is some truth to this response, sociologically speaking. Still, one might ask whether those accused of crimes who are wealthier, white, female, or males living in the more metropolitan north, are more likely to be innocent? Or might the "not so blind" judicial system offer them more opportunities for counsel, better counsel, and greater access to the appeals process? If one is poor, black or hispanic, male, and living in certain states, one's chances of getting a fair trial with decent counsel seem to be severely diminished, when compared with other defendants similarly charged. Is there not a subtle racist and discriminatory bias built into the judicial system in this country, and, if so, does this species of injustice offset or override the equitability or fairness of capital punishment as a viable tool of just retribution?

Q. **92. If discrimination and inequity are so prevalent, what would be the Christian approach to reforming the penal system?**

Not only could the penal system benefit from reform, but so too the whole criminal justice system—from police, through the judiciary and appeals process, to the actual prisons and rehabilitation facilities and programs available post-conviction. But I would like to suggest that efforts at reform, while needed and commendable, are more of a bandaid solution, the proverbial attempt to close the barn door once the horses already have fled. Why do people commit crimes? Why do people commit violent crimes? Yes, in some very basic sense, people are responsible for their own anger, their own malice, and their own choices of action. But aren't some people pushed toward a life of crime by poverty, or by their experience of prejudice, or by lack of education and job opportunities? It seems to me that attacking the problem of crime at the police and judicial end, while necessary, is costing too much and is often too late to do any real rehabilitative good. Would it not be better to attack the root social causes that lead many into the world of gangs, drugs, violence, and sexual assault?

This is not a Pollyanna plea. Tough social problems or sins require equally tough personal and community responses. But I think we, as Christians, are called to walk the extra mile, to turn the other cheek where possible, and to strive to build a better civil community, one more in keeping with the reign of God that Jesus inaugurated. By enhancing the access of the "last and least" among us to life's basics—food, shelter, clothing, healthcare, and the education necessary to garner living-wage jobs—we forestall a life of violence and crime for many. Will others choose the seemingly easy road in spite of our best social efforts? Sure. Jesus acknowledged that "the gate is wide and the road is easy that leads to destruction, and there are many [unfortunately] who take it" (Matt. 7:13).

Will some people who have all sorts of advantages still opt for a life of crime and amassing ill-gotten gain? Yes. Original sin still infects each of us and for some that means a choice to forgo healthy and holy opportunities in order to choose unwise and immoral ways. Our challenge is not to coerce everyone into model behavior but to create a society in which no one is forcibly left out or down-trodden. Thus, any reasonable and effective reform of the criminal justice system will also include targeting the causes of poverty and crime and sincerely attempting—personally, through the private sector, and with government help—to create a more humane, oppor-tunity-laden, well-policed, and fairly adjudicated community.

Q. **93. What does Christianity have to say about gun control and the legal ban on assault weapons?**

I'm glad you asked this question. When I was a child I took rifle practice and safety lessons at a university target range under the auspices of the National Rifle Association (NRA). At that time the reputation of that organization was impeccable, primarily as an advocate for safe hunting and the responsible use of firearms. How-ever, in the intervening decades the NRA seems to have evolved into a lobbying organization to champion the right to own and bear any and all manner of weapons. While in no way denying that the right to bear arms is included in the Bill of Rights lest any future govern-ment seek to disarm the populace for ulterior, dictatorial motives, I do think that the defense and advocacy of this right, seemingly with-out limits, is now grossly out of proportion to other basic rights and is a real threat to the common good.

It is hard for me to envision followers of Jesus amassing arsenals of weaponry, including assault rifles, automatic pistols, and armor-piercing bullets, as well as machine guns, bazookas, and other implements of large-scale destruction. It is ludicrous to label these as hunting weapons and scary to admit that one loves to collect them as a hobby, purely for the "enjoyment" of it. I find it inconsistent for followers of the Prince of Peace to relish collecting or using weapons that exceed any reasonable definition of a target pistol or hunting rifle. Add to this the fact that such weapons find their way so easily into the hands of common street criminals and gangs, and I think it is fair to say that the "right to bear arms" is out of control, certainly disproportionate to the society's right to protect the innocent from harm.

The old cliche that "guns don't kill people, people do" rings hollow. The vast majority of homicides each year, whether accidental or intentional, occur within families and often involve firearms. The easy availability of guns as well as their rather casual display and use contributes to the many lethal mishaps and killings done in the heat of the moment by family members or friends. If these deadly weapons were not so close at hand, one might have time to cool down before reacting. And there would be fewer accidental shootings if there were no loaded firearms.

I know of no mainline Christian church that supports the present state of affairs. There is rightful room for discussion about how to curb the sale and use of firearms, but I do not think that followers of Jesus or even non-Christians of good will can accept the status quo as humane, healthy, or morally justified. It seems to me that the NRA has crossed the boundary of civility and good sense by overemphasizing one civil right at the expense of others and to the detriment of the common good. While I respect their legal right to lobby for their cause and to spend vast sums of money doing so, I find their cause unjust and immoral. Although there is room for debate about weapons and civilian disarmament, I do not think one can rightly uphold the present stalemate.

Q. **94. You mentioned domestic violence. How should Christians deal with this problem?**

One can hardly pick up a daily newspaper or watch television news without seeing another report of domestic violence, most often of physical, sexual, and verbal abuse by a man perpetrated on his wife, girlfriend, or children. In a statement in 1991 on domestic violence, the United Church of Christ noted:

Among the many forms of violence, domestic violence has a special poignancy. The intimacy, interdependence, and vulnerability of persons within families leads to some of the most treasured human experiences. Here persons may find their greatest human security. But the same intimacy, interdependence, and vulnerability too often leads to great perils. . . . Specialists who have guided [our] inquiry into domestic violence tell us that "we live in an age of abuse." Violence is a "way of life in American culture."

This question and response should be read in tandem with question 59, in which we explored a healthy equality and mutuality between male and female, masculine and feminine. Enough genetic and hormonal evidence has been gathered to confirm that males, by nature and by cultural conditioning, tend to be more aggressive, more physical, and more violent. In recent classroom and workshop encounters with college-age young men, I have been surprised, even shocked, by the blatant male chauvinism and antifeminist backlash expressed. Comments like "men are meant to be in control, to act rather than discuss, and to take what they want" or "women are too emotional to be in leadership roles" were expressed far too often and with far too much vehemence to be overlooked as exceptions.

It is prudent to acknowledge basic male tendencies, whether biological or culturally encouraged, and the need to channel one's male ego and energy, as the current men's movement attempts to do. However, to baptize the dark side of some of these tendencies—aggressiveness rather than assertiveness, dominating control rather than steadfast commitment, and brute force rather than channeled physical strength—is to give license to abusive behavior either as if that's the way it's meant to be or under the rubric of "I can't help myself." Too many abusive relationships, marriages, and family situations involve this kind of masculinity gone awry.

At the same time, some women have a tendency to assume that their perceptions are either the right way to see things or automatically the universal norm. Women too can be self-absorbed, manipulative, aggressive, belittling, and insensitive in their own way. In rare instances a man may be their target or victim, but more often it is children, fellow employees, or others within their charge or care. Still, the predominant pattern in far too many family situations is an abusive male, a passive or submissive female, and children wrongly held to blame or accountability beyond their age or maturity.

Christian and humane virtues—love, patience, forgiveness, mercy, cooperation, and toleration—are needed. In many instances of domestic violence, all parties involved could use some primary lessons in self-esteem and affirmation. If we are to love others "as we love ourselves," then we'd better have a fairly healthy appreciation of self to serve as the model and measure for our appreciation and love of others (Mark 12:31; Matt. 22:39; Luke 10:27).

Many individuals and families involved in abusive relationships are unable to break their downward spiral or destructive patterns without outside intervention. Calling the police, seeking the help of competent social workers and pastoral care professionals, securing restraining orders, or moving to a safer environment (with other family members or to shelters for battered spouses or children)— these are some of the essential, but risky steps on the road to recovery. Where alcohol or drugs are involved, Alcoholics Anonymous, Al-Anon, and other Twelve Step programs or in-patient treatment centers may be invaluable resources. Admitting the problem and taking the first step—seeking help—are no small matters. To break an abusive cycle requires tremendous *faith* in yourself, *hope* that the future can be better, and the *courage* to make that first call or to move to a safe haven. Always know that God is never far from those who suffer and who are seeking a way out, a path to redemption and new life.

Q. **95. I feel funny asking this question here, rather than with the sexuality questions raised earlier, but it seems to fit. Is divorce ever the morally justified, Christian thing to do?**

There is probably no "right place" to ask questions about divorce. Divorce is tragic, and it doesn't neatly "fit" anywhere. It's not primarily a sexual question. It certainly has biblical roots and social implications. Given the fact that we have just dealt with abusive marriages and families, maybe this is the best place to speak about those "what if" situations.

The Roman Catholic approach to separation and divorce finds its roots in Jesus' own discussion of the subject in the Gospels of Mark and Luke. Some Pharisees tried to test Jesus by asking whether it is lawful for a man to divorce his wife. After soliciting from them an affirmative answer, based on the Mosaic Law (Deut. 24:1–4), Jesus explained that Moses allowed divorce because of their hardness of heart. He responds: "But from the beginning of creation, 'God made them male and female.' 'For this reason a man shall leave his father and mother and be joined to his wife, and the two shall become one flesh.' Therefore, what God has joined together, let no one separate" (Mark 10:6–9). Alone with his disciples, Jesus explained this even more bluntly: "Whoever divorces his wife and marries another commits adultery against her; and if she divorces her husband and marries another, she commits adultery" (Mark 10:11–12; Luke 16:18).

Contrary to Jewish custom, Jesus made it an equal offense for *either* spouse to divorce *and to marry another.* And so, across the centuries, the Roman Catholic tradition has condoned marital separation (if the severity of the situation called for it) as well as civil proceedings (now commonly known as "divorce") for the sake of legal matters, but has consistently forbidden these individuals to seek new partners. Why? Because in theory and in spirit they are still bound to their first mate by covenant promises "until death do us part." Having to live separately but without the freedom to marry again is the down-side of their pledge of fidelity "for better or worse."

What the Catholic church considers immoral is not the reality that some married couples, regrettably and tragically, ought not to live together anymore. What is considered "objectively wrong" is to seek another mate or spouse as long as one's first spouse, albeit separated, is still alive. Here one must remember that this person's subjective sincerity qualifies his or her moral responsibility or potential guilt. There are also moral questions about actions or omissions earlier in the marriage that may have contributed to this final separation. In irreconcilable or abusive situations, separation may well be the lesser evil, the best option, and therefore morally right. So also, filing for civil divorce to establish custody and property rights may also be necessary and morally understandable.

There is provision within Catholic church law for some marriages to be annulled, provided that certain prenuptial conditions or irregularities were present. According to church teaching, one's legal and valid civil marriage may not have met all the requirements essential for it to be considered a sacramental marriage. The church acknowledges that the legal (and breakable) civil contract of marriage was not, in certain instances, an indissoluble covenant marriage "till death do us part." In these cases, once an annulment has been decreed, a person is free to marry. The topic of church annulments is less a matter for us in this moral discussion than for one to take up with one's pastor, parish minister, or a church lawyer.

Again, given that this is a book about *Christian morality*, and not solely its Roman Catholic expression, there is an alternative view concerning divorce and remarriage. In Matthew's Gospel we find a slightly altered version of Jesus' saying about divorce. Matthew's Jesus builds in one exception to the prohibition against divorce: "And I say to you, whoever divorces his wife, except for unchastity, and marries another commits adultery [and he who marries a divorced woman commits adultery]" (Matt. 19:9; 5:32). This so-called Matthean exception, *unchastity* (sometimes translated *adultery*), has been adopted by most Protestant and Orthodox Christians as an illustration of Jesus, or the early church of Matthew, granting a pastoral exception to the marriage ideal. Rather than seeing marriage as absolutely indissoluble, these other Christian communities recognize, appreciate, and adopt Matthew's single allowance for divorce. St. Paul made a somewhat parallel exception for early Christians who were tied to abusive unbelieving (pagan) spouses (1 Cor. 7:12–16).

Given Martin Luther's deep sense of human sinfulness as well as his great confidence in God's redemptive mercy, he set the pattern for other Protestant communities who have been more tolerant of human frailty and sin, even within marriage. Their allowance for second marriages, particularly in the case where a wife had been betrayed, has served women and their children well, particularly in cultures where single women have or had little access to jobs or a living wage. While Catholic scripture scholar Joseph Fitzmyer disputes whether the exception clause in Matthew refers to "infidelity" and "adultery," it has generally been accepted by most New Testament scholars across the centuries, particularly those of the Protestant and Orthodox traditions.

In either case, whether the more restrictive Catholic approach or the more accepting wider Christian stance, divorce is a sad event. Still, in certain tragic marital situations—ongoing spouse and/or child abuse being the most blatant—separation and "civil divorce" are surely no sin. It may well be the safest and sanest option for all concerned, the lesser evil, the morally right thing to do. The question of subsequent marriage remains a point of Christian tension, with Catholics resorting to possible annulments, while other Christians more readily accept that the spouses, no longer tied to each other, may be free to marry.

PART SIX

Forgiveness, Fidelity, and Faith

Q. 96. I've heard that there is one sin that is "unforgivable." Is that true? And if so, what is the "unforgivable sin"?

I think you may be referring to the "sin" mentioned by Jesus in the Gospels: "Truly I tell you, people will be forgiven for their sins and whatever blasphemies they utter, but whoever blasphemes against the Holy Spirit can never have forgiveness, but is guilty of an eternal sin" (Mark 3:28–29; Matt. 12:32; Luke 12:10). That sounds pretty final. If there ever were a definition of "mortal sin," this would seem to be it. All too often this passage and the "unforgivable sin" are raised by very scrupulous people, basically good people who are caught up with worries and self-doubts, fearing that deep down they may be wicked or damned. Often such scrupulosity is rooted in childhood fears or in past religious experiences that portrayed God as angry or vengeful. Such people are to be treated with great kindness and mercy. Mere logic is often inadequate to help them work through their scrupulosity. Often they need professional psychological counseling to recover their equilibrium and a better sense of God, neighbor, and self.

In referring to the "unforgivable sin" the *Catechism of the Catholic Church* affirms that God's mercy is limitless. God's desire and capacity to forgive exceed all bounds. However, if a person deliberately and obstinately refuses to repent and accept such divine mercy, it is possible that they may be rejecting not only the forgiveness of their sins but salvation itself (#1864). Still, Christians have always affirmed that where sin abounds, grace abounds more (Rom. 5:20). God's infinite mercy outdistances our ability to sin. So the only possibility that, in some sense, *might* trump God's forgiveness would be

143

for us finally, definitively, and for all time to reject God's abiding presence and offer of mercy. Deathbed conversions attest to God's patience and willingness to wipe the slate clean, even in our final moments of life.

To those who worry about the *unforgivable sin* and whether they might have committed it, I usually respond, "Relax, if you're still worried about it and whether you've offended God or not, then you haven't committed it. You still care and that, ultimately, is the sign of your abiding faith." God's infinite mercy exceeds all our scrupulous apprehensions and inordinate fears.

Q. **97. Speaking of forgiveness, are we obliged always to "forgive and forget"?**

It is interesting that the scriptures don't speak much about forgetting past wrongs, whether our own or those committed against us. We can learn from past mistakes. Experience is a great teacher. So too, wounds from past sins and broken relationships can and do scab over and eventually heal, but often they leave a psychic scar. As the old cliche goes, "it is better to have loved and lost, than never to have loved at all." Often we are "sadder but wiser" in the distant aftermath of hurtful and/or sinful experiences. So while we may never forget the feelings and some of the memories of past hurts, we are called to rise above those and to be merciful, to forgive others in the same generous way that we have been forgiven by God.

How often must we forgive others? Peter thought he was being big-hearted by suggesting "seven times." Jesus challenged Peter, and by extension us, to go the extra mile: "Not seven times, but, I tell you, seventy times seven times" (Matt. 18:21–22). God's merciful forgiveness knows no bounds. We are called to echo and incarnate that same bounty to the best of our frail, yet graced human ability. Often, this kind of forgiving attitude takes time. Forgiveness is more of a process than a single event.

The call to "love our enemies" and to "pray for those who persecute us" does not mean that we agree with them, or enjoy their company, or necessarily wish to encounter them again in the future. Following a divorce or a major breach in a friendship or if we have lost a loved one due to some criminal's action, we may never feel good about that person again. But we can "let go" of our bitterness and harsh judgments. We can pray for them. We can allow healing to take place within us and that, to some degree, involves wishing the other person well. "Farewell" is an interesting word. Literally it means "fare thee well," that is, I strive to bear you no ill will (for your sake and for mine); may you fare well, now, and in the future.

Q. **98. As you look around the world today, is there one moral issue that you think is most important or is being neglected most?**

At the risk of getting on my soapbox to preach, I honestly think that what our society could use most today is an infusion of the virtue of *fidelity*. One also might call it *commitment, personal integrity, promise keeping,* or *fortitude*. When we have the virtue of courage, we can do the right thing or rise to the occasion at the moment. But when we have the virtue of fortitude, we are courageous *over the long haul.*

I think long-term fidelity is in too short supply in our world. Too many marriages break up and often they're abandoned too soon, before the partners have given it that extra mile and have turned the other cheek. Too many people leave the priesthood, the ministry, or forgo their solemn religious vows. Friendships that last a lifetime, that can withstand a major quarrel or misunderstanding, are too rare today. At one point in time a person's word was his or her bond. Promise keeping and oath taking were viewed as binding now and for the future. More often today someone promises to keep a secret or confidence and all too quickly they are telling someone else about it "in strictest confidence." Even in terms of work commitments, management too often gouges labor, overriding binding contract agreements, while labor undermines management, threatening to strike or to bring the company to its knees. Are we people who keep our contracts, our commitments, our covenant relationships, our solemn word?

Recently, I was privileged to watch the parents of a close friend of mine wage a year-long battle against cancer. Through all those months, both before and after hospice came on the scene, Andy gently and dutifully cared for Margaret. He took care of her most intimate, personal, and embarrassing needs. In the end, after the funeral, Andy—with tears in his eyes, but a smile on his face—said, "I did it. I kept my word. I swore to her on our wedding day that I'd be there until death do us part. I never imagined it would be like this. I thought we'd grow old together and some morning one of us just wouldn't wake up. I never anticipated a long battle with cancer. But I swore to her I'd be there, *and I did it!* She'd have been there for me, so *I had to* be there for her." Now that is covenant commitment, that is fidelity, that is fortitude (i.e., courage over the long haul).

I mean no disrespect to those people who sincerely believe they must leave a marriage or forsake some prior commitment. There surely are understandable pastoral exceptions to the promise-keeping norm. Discerning whether further efforts at reconciliation are warranted or not requires personal honesty, prudent counsel, prayerful openness, and a measure of humility. But I think too often too many of us bail out too soon. If you ask me which of the virtues we all need to practice more these days, I am firmly convinced that it is *fidelity* to our word.

Q. **99. What do you say to those of us who might have wayward children or relatives, loved ones who have wandered from the "straight and narrow" path of moral or spiritual righteousness?**

Many parents, brothers or sisters, and close relatives worry about family members or friends who have "gone astray." When young people first leave home, often they flirt with a looser life-style. They sometimes forgo regular church attendance. They may stretch their wings a bit, morally speaking, and flirt with evil. Some choose to forsake the values their parents taught them or, more often, they slip into bad practices and patterns of vice that are hard to break. In the same way, middle-aged friends or older loved ones may react badly to a crisis, a major loss, or a misunderstanding. Estrangement knows no boundaries of age, race, religion, or ethnic group. I offer here two simple pieces of advice: (1) Don't be self-righteous. And (2) Be patient.

Try not to be self-righteous. Try not to sit in harsh judgment. Never disown or abandon or forsake the prodigal son, daughter, parent, or friend. The father of the prodigal son not only mirrors

God's abiding mercy, but also ought to be a model for us who wait and pray for a loved one gone astray: "But while [the boy] was still far off, his father saw him and was filled with compassion; he ran and put his arms around him and kissed him [tenderly]" (Luke 15:20). There is a fine line between coddling a wrongdoer, seeming to show approval for their misdeeds, and being firm but not self-righteous. People may need our challenge but not our disdain. They may benefit from our exhortation but not our condemnation. Getting in touch with our own anger and wrath, our own regret and guilt, may allow us to be more humble and less judgmental.

My mother is fond of the old saying, "Patience is a virtue, possess it if you can." Some of us live rather structured and punctual lives. We don't like messiness. We tend to be prompt and are uncomfortable with things being left undone, unresolved. The Christian tradition assures us that God is less rigid, less bound by time and space. God is patient. We have a lifetime in which to learn to practice virtue. God has all eternity in which to create, encourage, cajole, inspire, bless, and forgive. Seeing a loved one being self-destructive or hurting others is often painful for us. But I encourage you to be patient. God works in mysterious ways across one's life span. At any given moment God is not finished creating us and helping us to refine and recreate ourselves. Like the parent of the prodigal son, may we be watching and waiting, full of compassion, trusting in God's grace to work, in God's good time.

Q. **100. How would you sum up the meaning of "Christian morality"?**

Ninety-nine questions ago I defined *morality* as "one's values, choices, and actions." We each create our own hybrid morality or ethical code from the values and virtues espoused by the various communities to which we belong. Those of us who are *Christian* draw special meaning from the story of a divine love affair, the ongoing covenant commitment between God and all of humanity. Jesus of Nazareth is the centerpiece of that story. His life, death, resurrection, and ongoing presence in the Spirit give meaning to our daily lives. "Loving God, neighbor, and self" is a thumbnail expression of that faith story. God is there with us every step of the way—

empowering, encouraging, inspiring, exhorting, and, when needed, forgiving. Our challenge is to accept that grace, to allow it to transform our lives, and to make it real by sharing it with others. This is our morality, our distinctively Christian "values, choices, and actions."

Again and again in the Gospels we find Jesus calling people to *conversion* or *metanoia*. The term literally means a "turnaround." When we sin, particularly when we do mortal or serious wrong, we "miss the mark" by more than a few degrees. Sadly, we sometimes choose to go in the opposite direction from Christ, who is and ought to be our way, truth, and life. When we stray, we are called to *metanoia*, to turn around, to get back on track, to get going in the right direction again.

Conversion or *metanoia* is not usually an instantaneous event. A few of us may be like St. Paul, who got knocked to the ground, called to an immediate "turnaround" in his life and way of thinking. But many of us, perhaps most of us, are more like St. Peter, whose faith and moral life seemed to have peaks and valleys, whose conversion seemed to be a bit cyclical and ongoing. One moment he was professing undying fidelity, and the next moment he was denying the Lord three times. One moment he was unwilling to eat with Gentile converts and the next moment he was proclaiming that God shows no partiality in calling people to faith.

Christian morality is ultimately the story of conversion, the lifelong process of "being" and "doing"–*being* the children of God and disciples of Christ whom we profess to be, by *doing* those loving actions which further God's reign here on earth. And practice does indeed help to make us perfect, or at least closer to perfection than when we first began this conversion process. *Who we are,* as daughters and sons of God, spills over into *what we do;* and *what we do,* in the name of Christ Jesus, helps to make us *who we are.* It's as simple and complex as that. Jesus came that we "may have life, and have it abundantly" (John 10:10). May it be so for you, for me, and for all people, now and evermore.

Suggestions for Further Reading

Part One
Definitions and Moral Decision Making

Catechism of the Catholic Church (1994). Part 3: "Life In Christ" (pp. 421–611). Various publishers.

Crook, Roger. *An Introduction to Christian Ethics*. Englewood Cliffs, N.J.: Prentice Hall, 1990.

Lucker, Raymond, et al. *The People's Catechism: Catholic Faith for Adults*. New York: Crossroad, 1995.

McBrien, Richard P. *Catholicism*, New Edition (Completely Revised and Updated). New York: Harper, 1994. Part 6: "Christian Morality" (pp. 881–1014).

Overberg, Kenneth, S.J. *Conscience in Conflict: How to Make Moral Choices*. Cincinnati: St. Anthony Messenger Press, 1991.

Part Two
Issues in Healthcare Ethics

Flynn, Eileen. *Your Living Will: Why, When and How to Write One*. New York: Citadel Press, 1992.

Kelly, David. *Critical Care Ethics: Treatment Decisions in American Hospitals*. Kansas City: Sheed & Ward, 1991.

McCarthy, Jeremiah, and Judith Caron. *Medical Ethics: A Catholic Guide to Healthcare Decisions*. Liguori, Mo.: Liguori, 1990.

Nelson, James B., and JoAnne Smith Rohricht. *Human Medicine*. Minneapolis: Augsburg, 1984. A bit dated, but well done.

Sparks, Richard C. *To Treat or Not to Treat: Bioethics and the Handicapped Newborn*. Mahwah, N.J.: Paulist Press, 1988.

149

Thomas, Leo, and Jan Alkire. *Healing as a Parish Ministry*. Notre Dame: Ave Maria Press, 1992.

Part Three
Issues in Sexual Morality

Hanigan, James. *What Are They Saying About Sexual Morality?* Mahwah, N.J.: Paulist Press, 1982. Rev. ed., forthcoming.

National Conference of Catholic Bishops. *Human Sexuality: A Catholic Perspective for Education and Lifelong Learning*. Washington, D.C.: U.S.C.C. Publications, 1991.

Nelson, James B. *Body Theology*. Louisville: Westminster/John Knox, 1992.

Whitehead, Evelyn, and James Whitehead. *A Sense of Sexuality: Christian Love and Intimacy*. New York: Doubleday, 1989.

Part Four
Issues in Political and Economic Life

Episcopal Church in America. *Economic Justice and the Christian Conscience*. Commended by the House of Bishops, 1987.

Kammer, Fred. *Doing Faithjustice*. Mahwah, N.J.: Paulist Press, 1991.

Lutheran Church in America. *Economic Justice–Stewardship of Creation in Human Community*. Adopted by the 10th Biennial Convention, 1980.

National Conference of Catholic Bishops. *Economic Justice for All*. Washington, D.C.: U.S.C.C. Publications, 1986.

United Presbyterian Church, USA. *Christian Faith and Economic Life*. Study Guide Approved by the General Assembly, 1984.

Part Five
Issues in Peacemaking, Capital Punishment, and Violence

John Paul II. *The Gospel of Life*. An encyclical letter "On the Value and Inviolability of Human Life." Washington, D.C.: U.S.C.C. Publications, 1995.

National Conference of Catholic Bishops. *The Challenge of Peace: God's Promise and Our Response.* Washington, D.C.: U.S.C.C. Publications, 1983.

Overberg, Kenneth, S.J. "The Death Penalty: Why the Church Speaks a Countercultural Message." *Catholic Update* #CO195 (January 1995). Cincinnati: St. Anthony Messenger Press, 1995.

United Methodist Council of Bishops. *In Defense of Creation: The Nuclear Crisis and a Just Peace.* Nashville: Graded Press, 1986.

Part Six
Forgiveness, Fidelity, and Faith

Farley, Margaret. *Personal Commitments: Beginning, Keeping, Changing.* San Francisco: Harper & Row, 1986, 1990.

Garrity, Robert. *O Happy Fault: Personal Recovery Through Spiritual Growth.* Mahwah, N.J.: Paulist Press, 1994.

Himes, Michael. *Doing the Truth in Love: Conversations about God, Relationships, and Service.* Mahwah, N.J.: Paulist Press, 1995.

O'Keefe, Mark. *Becoming Good, Becoming Holy.* Mahwah, N.J.: Paulist Press, 1995.

Index

OF RELATED INTEREST

 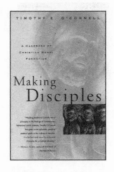 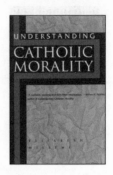

Charles Shelton, S.J.
ACHIEVING MORAL HEALTH
An Exercise Plan for Your Conscience

Although it is common knowledge that a person's physical health improves with regular exercise, many often do not think that moral health also requires commitment and attention. This book offers a timely exploration of the ways in which our conscience can develop—and, further, provides a set of exercises to facilitate this important growth.

0-8245-1868-3, $18.95 paperback

Timothy E. O'Connell
MAKING DISCIPLES
A Handbook of Christian Moral Formation

Answers from theology, psychology, and sociology to the question: How do people actually come to embody Christian values, and what does this learning mean for church and ministry? O'Connell has "made complex research eminently accessible and has offered us immediate applications of that research…"—WILLIAM J. BAUSCH

0-8245-1727-X, $21.95, paperback

Elizabeth L. Willems
UNDERSTANDING CATHOLIC MORALITY
This concise and well-written text focuses on development, not simply the acquisition of learning about Catholic morality. An ideal addition for personal or classroom study.

0-8245-1725-3, $19.95 paperback

OF RELATED INTEREST

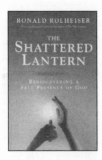
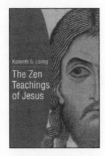

Ronald Rolheiser
THE SHATTERED LANTERN
Rediscovering a Felt Presence of God

The way back to a lively faith "is not a question of finding the right answers, but of living a certain way. The existence of God, like the air we breathe, need not be proven…"

Rolheiser shines new light on the contemplative path of Western Christianity and offers a dynamic way forward.

0-8245-1884-5, $14.95 paperback

Kenneth S. Leong
THE ZEN TEACHINGS OF JESUS

"I left Jesus to search for the Tao when I was sixteen," writes Kenneth Leong. "Now I am forty and realize that I could have found the Tao in Jesus." It is the spiritual side of Zen, the art to trust and accept life that coincides with the core of the Gospel message.

0-8245-1883-7, $19.95 paperback

Robert Barron
AND NOW I SEE
A Theology of Transformation

"Barron…elucidates the meaning of salvation for Christians by examining the change of heart and consciousness that comes with *metanoia,* the Greek term whose full impact is lost in translation as 'repentance.'"—LIBRARY JOURNAL

0-8245-1753-9, $19.95 paperback

Please support your local bookstore, or call 1-800-707-0670.

For a free catalog, please write us at:
The Crossroad Publishing Co.,
481 Eighth Avenue, Suite 1550, New York, NY 10001
www.crossroadpublishing.com